JUDGE
YOUR OWN
HORSEMANSHIP

Neale Haley

Arco Publishing Company, Inc.
New York

Published by ARCO PUBLISHING COMPANY, Inc.
219 Park Avenue South, New York, N.Y. 10003

First ARCO Edition, 1974

Library of Congress Catalog Card Number 74-76850
ISBN 0-668-03410-6

Printed in the United States of America

Preface

How to Use This Book

The tests that are the basis of this book have been designed so that you may use them to judge your own proficiency as a rider. They may also be used to help you judge other riders in horse shows. An entire horse show may be set up and judged on the basis of the skills outlined in each section.

In each of the four sections of this book the tests are arranged from the easiest to the most difficult, beginning with the White Ribbon Tests and progressing through the Yellow, Red and Blue. You should begin testing yourself with the first test you are able to pass easily. As you practice the skills outlined in the succeeding tests, you will gradually be able to pass each one until you have reached the advanced level.

The important sections in each of the tests are starred. You should be able to pass these sections with assurance before you begin working on the next test. The White and Yellow Ribbon Tests in each section are much easier than the Red and Blue Ribbon Tests. Always allow more days of practice for the more difficult tests than you do for the easier ones. You should pass the Red and Blue Tests with a high degree of skill.

The horsemanship sections teach you background knowledge and things you should know about horses at each level of advancement. Many of the questions listed are asked by judges in horse shows before final decisions about ribbons are made.

This test system can be used for groups of riders. Instructors should be particularly careful about passing riders on Blue Ribbon Tests, since these advance a student to more difficult classes and more intensive competition. You need to be certain the student will be able to cope with the more advanced work. The White Ribbon Tests for intermediates and advanced riders include some review to assist the student in consolidating his gains from previous lessons.

Instructors may also use this book to divide classes in horse shows. Your show can include students who are learning to ride as well as those on an advanced level. It is often helpful to your judge to know the skills the riders in each class have mastered and to use a check list for judging based on the tests the riders have taken. Your students, too, may use the tests to judge mock horse shows among themselves. This helps them recognize the importance of each skill they are learning, and how to improve their own riding.

Contents

Acknowledgments

Ideas are the most precious things a person can be given. Many have contributed their ideas to make this book a success. For her unusual approach and skilled fingers, I wish to thank Marge Kinley who did the drawings for the tests. For her ideas on riding, her willingness to answer a hundred questions and all her help in making this book possible, my thanks to Margie Schaltauer. Both Tom and Linda Kranz, as camp directors, have proved these tests practical and contributed their own ideas as to how they might be improved. For her clear way of expressing ideas and new concepts in how to jump, my thanks to Kim Haley. Many of the basic ideas of how to ride well have come from Doug Haley.

I also wish to acknowledge the contributions of Louise Kirtland and Julia Westphal.

Above all, my gratitude to Jacqueline Kranz, who has so often supplied the horses, encouragement and practical solutions to problems that have made these tests so useful to hundreds of children.

Part I

TESTS FOR BEGINNING RIDERS

1

White Ribbon Test

Riding section:

1. Demonstrate how to mount a horse correctly. Which way do you face? What do you do with your hands?
2. Demonstrate how to dismount correctly.
*3. Demonstrate the correct way to hold your reins. Where should your hands be when you are riding?
4. Show how to stop a horse.
5. Show how to go around the corner in a ring.
*6. How do you make a horse walk or trot without kicking him?
*7. Trot your horse. You may use the trotting (galloping) position.

Question section:

1. Locate: pommel, stirrup, stirrup leather, bit, withers, croup, head, back.
2. Explain how a rider should approach a horse.
3. On which side do you mount?
4. Why do you face the rear of the horse when you mount?
5. Why should a rider hold the reins when he mounts even if someone else is holding the horse?

6. Why do you avoid kicking a horse to make him go, although, if he is stubborn, you kick him hard?

7. Why do you shorten the reins before you stop a horse?

HOW TO JUDGE YOUR PROFICIENCY ON THE WHITE RIBBON TEST

Riding section:

1. The important points to remember when you mount a horse:
   - Take the reins in your left hand *before* you start to mount.
   - Your right hand rests across the pommel.
   - Face the rear of your horse.
   - When you swing onto him, you should jump and swing up in one movement so that your right leg swings clear across his back without touching him.
   - You should sit down gently in the saddle.

Common mistakes:
   - Be sure you do not kick your horse in the side or on the croup.
   - You must not let go of the reins.
   - You should not tug so hard on the saddle that you pull it awry.
   - It hurts the horse if you sit down with a thump on his back.
   - You should not put your right hand under the middle of the front of the saddle.
   - Your right knee should not bend while you swing your leg across the croup.

While you are mounting your movements should be quiet and steady, rather than jerky. Mounting correctly depends more on balance than on jumping hard and tugging on the mane and saddle. The two worst mistakes you can make are to let go of the reins and to kick your horse accidentally.

2. The points to remember when you dismount:
   • You should hold both reins and part of the mane in your left hand.
   • Your right hand should rest on the front of the saddle during the entire dismount.
   • Your right leg should swing high over your horse's croup.
   • You should be balanced on your hands when you take your left foot out of the stirrup.

Common mistakes:
   • You should not shift your right hand to the back of the saddle in the middle of dismounting.
   • You should not lean across the saddle in order to take your left foot out of the stirrup.
   • You should be careful not to jerk on the reins while you are dismounting.
   • Even as a beginner you should be able to balance on your hands, with your elbows straight, in order to take your left foot out of the stirrup. Since the reins control the horse, it is a major mistake to drop them while you dismount.

If you hurt your horse either by kicking him accidentally or tugging on his mouth, you should count this part of the test as a failure.

3. When you hold the reins correctly, they come up through your palms so that your baby fingers on the reins are closer to the horse's mouth than your thumbs are. One rein is in each hand. The ends of the reins are flipped over your fingers and your thumb holds each end in place.

Your hands should be a few inches apart, in front of the saddle, and held slightly above your horse's withers.

Common mistakes:
- The ends of your reins should not stand up straight out of your fists.
- You should not hold your reins with your palms up and your thumbs closer to the horse's mouth than your baby fingers.
- Your hands should not be over the front of the saddle.
- Your reins should not be so tight that you are pulling on the bit.

4. When you are stopping a horse, you should shorten the reins first before you pull on them. Do not lean forward at the same time you pull, but "sit back." Do not let your heels go up as you pull.

5. You should pull on one rein only as you turn your horse around the corner of the ring.

6. A horse knows you want him to go faster
- If you squeeze with your legs,
- Put your weight forward,
- And "pick up"—shorten—your reins a little.

Common mistakes:
- You should not kick a horse until you have tried to make him go with leg pressure first.

- You should not lean back, let your heels go up, and try to make your horse move faster at the same time.
- If your reins are so tight you are pulling on the bit, you cannot make your horse move more quickly.

You need to think about your horse before you ask him to trot. Is he expecting you to change gaits? A sure sign of a beginner is someone who startles his horse by a sudden kick when his horse is half asleep. Always *ask* your horse to do something before you try to *make* him do what you want.

7. When you trot,
   - Be sure you stand up balanced in a trotting (galloping) position first. Your knees should be slightly bent, your heels down, your head up, your hands on the mane.
   - Your reins should be shorter than when you walk.
   - You should be relaxed as you trot.

Common mistakes:
   - You should not lean forward close to your horse's neck.
   - If your heels go up, you will fall forward on the neck.
   - If your legs swing forward, you will sit down in the saddle.
   - If you let go of the mane, you are likely to jerk on your horse's mouth.

You should not become tense when you trot. A good rider is able to relax in each skill he masters. It is more important to do each step in a test well, with confidence, than to do a more difficult test and feel tense as you do it.

Horsemanship section:

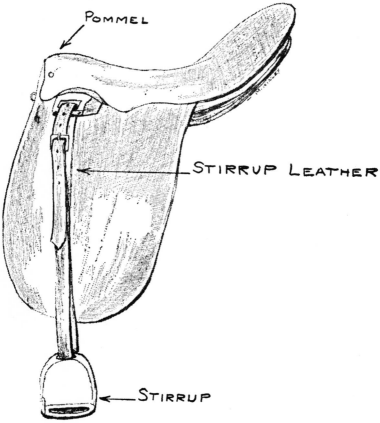

POMMEL

STIRRUP LEATHER

STIRRUP

Parts of the saddle

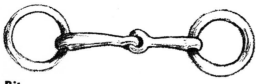

Bit

1. (See diagram) Parts of the saddle:

POMMEL: The raised front of the saddle.

STIRRUP: The metal iron where you put your foot.

STIRRUP LEATHER: The strap that can be lengthened or shortened to make your stirrups the correct length for you.

BIT: The part of the bridle that goes inside the horse's mouth.

Parts of the horse

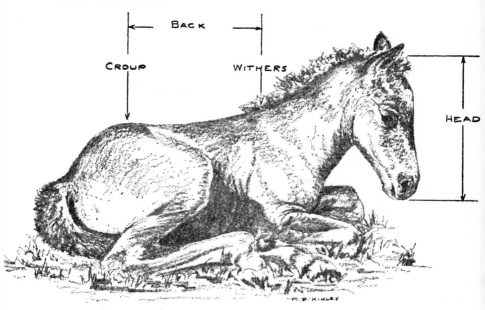

WITHERS: The bone at the base of the horse's neck; the highest part of the back of the horse.

CROUP: The rear end of the horse.

HEAD: This includes his long nose and back to his ears.

BACK: The middle of the horse from his withers to his croup.

2. A rider should always approach the horse quietly, from the front so the horse sees him. He should speak to the horse quietly as he approaches.

3. A rider mounts on the left side.

4. A rider faces the rear of his horse when he mounts so the horse cannot cow-kick. Also, if the horse steps forward, the movement helps a rider swing into the saddle. If the horse steps forward when a rider is facing the front, the rider is left behind.

5. You want control of your own horse when you are mounting. A friend who is holding your horse while you mount may suddenly let go because the horse has decided to sniff his arm and he is afraid of being bitten, or a fly has landed on your friend's nose—or for countless other reasons.

6. The more you kick a horse the less attention he pays to your heels. If you can make your horse go with leg pressure, he will have sensitive sides and respond to your training more readily. However, a stubborn horse must be kicked if he will not go. The kick should be hard enough for him to know you mean business. The next time you want him to go, he should walk or trot without a kick. A kick is a punishment and not the best way to make a horse move.

7. You shorten the reins before you stop so you do not have to pull your hands way back to your stomach or far out to either side in order to have leverage on the bit.

Yellow Ribbon Test

Riding section:

1. Demonstrate correct form when you are walking your horse.
2. In what way does this position change when you
    a. stop
    b. turn
3. Demonstrate a correct trotting (galloping) position.
*4. Trot around the ring in your trotting (galloping) position. Show how you keep your balance.
5. Show how to tell if your stirrups are the correct length.

Horsemanship section:

1. What is the purpose of learning a trotting (galloping) position?
2. Why should you keep your heels down while you are learning to ride?
3. Why should you keep your eyes up when you are riding?
4. What is the reason for sitting up straight on your horse?
5. Locate: cantle, tree, cheek bone, neck.
6. Does it hurt the horse to have his mane pulled?

HOW TO JUDGE YOUR PROFICIENCY ON THE YELLOW RIBBON TEST

Riding section:

1. Correct form when you are walking your horse means:
   - Your back is straight and erect.
   - Your head is up so that you are looking forward between your horse's ears.
   - Your hands are in front of the saddle and you are holding the reins correctly.
   - Your elbows are bent so that your arms are relaxed at your sides.
   - Your legs are underneath you. This means your stirrup leathers hang down straight. If you bend forward to look over your knee, you just see the tip of your boot.
   - The ball of your foot is on the stirrup.
   - Your knees are bent slightly.
   - Your heels are down and out of the horse's sides.

Common mistakes:
   - Slouching or crouching close to the horse's neck is a fault.
   - Beginning riders tend to look down too much to see what they are doing with the reins.
   - Your heels should not get higher than your toes; your foot should not slip "home" in the stirrup; your toes should not stick out at right angles to your horse.

If you begin riding with correct form you will develop the muscles you need to be a good rider, you will have balance, and proper form will become natural to you.

Whenever you ride, whether you are testing yourself or not, you should practice correct form.

2. Your position changes when you stop.
   • Your weight shifts back slightly.
   • You make sure you push into your heels even if your legs go forward a little.
   • You will be pulling on the reins, so your hands come closer to your body.

Common mistakes:
   • You should not lean forward when you pull on the reins.
   • Your heels should not go up, nor should your knees bend so that your legs swing backward.
   • You will lose control if you pull your arms up in the air.
   • Only your head and one hand move when you turn. You should look in the direction you are going and shorten the rein on that side.

3. When you stand in your trotting position:
   • Your reins are shortened.
   • Your hands are on the mane.
   • Your shoulders are further forward than your buttocks, but your back is still straight.
   • Your weight presses into your heels.
   • Your legs and feet are in the same position as when you are sitting in the saddle.
   • Your head is up; your eyes forward.

This is a basic position in riding. You should be able to stand in it easily, without being stiff or losing your balance.

4. When you trot in your trotting position you should feel secure and relaxed.

Common mistakes:

• Your heels should not ride up, because you will lose your balance, your thighs will come off the saddle (making you sloppy and insecure), and your legs will slide backward so that you fall forward on the horse's neck.

• You should not straighten your knees, because this makes you stiff, jars you as the horse trots, and often forces your legs to swing forward so that you sit down on the saddle.

• Your elbows should not be straight.

• Your reins should not be so tight that your horse's chin is tucked or his mouth open.

In order to pass this test you should be able to trot easily in your trotting position. You should be able to stay in it for five minutes or more without feeling tired and without pulling on your horse's mane to keep from losing your balance. Your horse should continue to trot without it being necessary to kick him over and over again.

5. Your stirrups are the correct length if you are able to take a trotting position and your body does not touch the front of the saddle. You should be able to keep your heels down and your knees bent slightly.

Horsemanship section:

1. A trotting or galloping position enables a rider to be balanced at a trot without posting. The position is also used for jumping.

2. You should keep your heels down when you are learning to ride because your weight is then on the stirrups.

When your heels are pushed down and away from the horse's sides, your thighs are pressed close to the saddle to make your seat secure.

3. Your eyes should be up when you ride so that you will be able to watch where you are going. Also, because your head is the heaviest part of your body, it affects your position and your balance. If your head is up, you are helping to keep your balance over the horse's point of balance.

4. A rider sits straight because it gives him a position of strength, yet leaves his body supple to move and turn with his horse.

5. (See diagram)

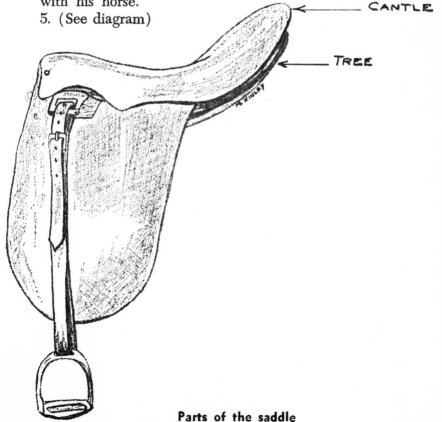

CANTLE

TREE

Parts of the saddle

CANTLE: The raised back of the saddle.

TREE: The core of the saddle on which the leather parts are built.

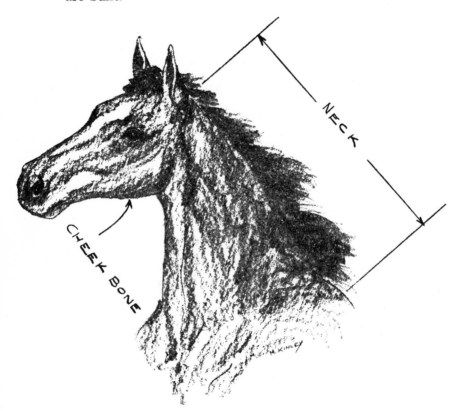

Parts of a horse's head

CHEEK BONE: The large bone on each side of the horse's head.

NECK: From his ears to his withers.

6. It does not hurt the horse to have you pull on his mane.

3
Red Ribbon Test

Riding section:

*1. Demonstrate your ability to post in rhythm while you are trotting with your hands on the mane.
*2. Demonstrate the correct way to stop your horse when the horse in front of you continues to trot.
3. Make an emergency dismount when your horse is standing still.

Horsemanship section:

1. Locate: girth, billets, skirt, throat latch, keepers.
2. When should you check your girth?
3. What is the use of the throat latch? of keepers?
4. Explain the correct way to lead a horse. Where should the rider hold the reins while he is leading his horse? On which side should he walk?
5. What should a rider do if his horse stumbles?

HOW TO JUDGE YOUR PROFICIENCY ON THE RED RIBBON TEST

1. When you post in rhythm with your horse:
   • Your posting is even, beat after beat.
   • Your legs are still and your heels stay down.
   • Your position is correct. When you sit in the saddle as you post, your position is the same as if you were walking your horse. At the top of your posting, your position is the same as your trotting position.
   • Your elbows bend and straighten as you post.
   • You are relaxed.

Common mistakes:
   • Your legs should not swing back and forth each time you post.
   • Your heels should not go up and down.
   • Your arms should not be stiff or your elbows straight.
   • You should not let go of the mane.
   • You should not need to pull on the mane to get out of the saddle to post.
   • You should not take a double bounce in the saddle.

The Red Ribbon Test for a beginner is judged primarily on your ability to post. Quiet, relaxed, effortless is the way your posting should be.

2. When you stop your horse at the same time another horse trots away in front of you
   • Your pull on the reins needs to be firm and strong.
   • Your reins should be short enough to make your horse stop and remain standing still.

Common mistakes:
- You should not jerk on the reins.
- Your reins should not be so long you cannot control your horse. If he refuses to stop, takes many steps to stop, or begins to walk as soon as he has stopped, you do not have control.
- If you continue to pull after he stops, rather than releasing as soon as he obeys, you are unkind to your horse and will develop hard hands. You are also training him incorrectly. He should always be rewarded for obedience.

3. When you make an emergency dismount
   - You must take your feet out of the stirrups *first*.
   - You should grab your horse around the neck and jump to the ground.
   - You should land facing the front of your horse.

Common mistakes:
- You should fail this test if you forget to take your feet out of the stirrups before you try to jump off your horse.
- You should not kick your horse as you jump off.
- You should not land with a thump on the ground.
- You should not let go of the reins.

Horsemanship section:

1. (See diagram)
   GIRTH: The leather, canvas or string strap that goes underneath your horse's stomach to hold the saddle in place.
   BILLETS: The straps on the saddle to which the girth is fastened.

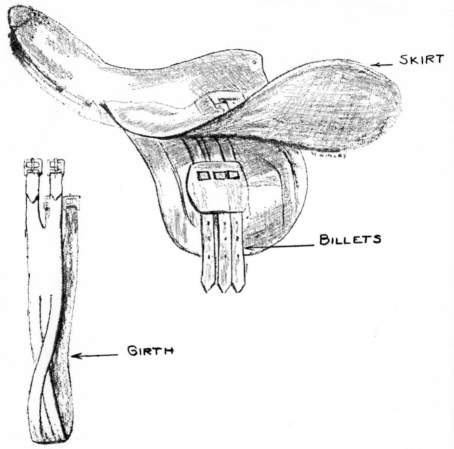

SKIRT

BILLETS

GIRTH

Parts of the saddle

SKIRT: The flap on the saddle that covers the billets.

THROAT LATCH: The narrow strap that passes under the horse's neck and holds the bridle on.

KEEPERS: The narrow bands that fit over the ends of straps to hold them in place, much as the loops on pants hold belts in place.

2. You should check your girth before you mount, after

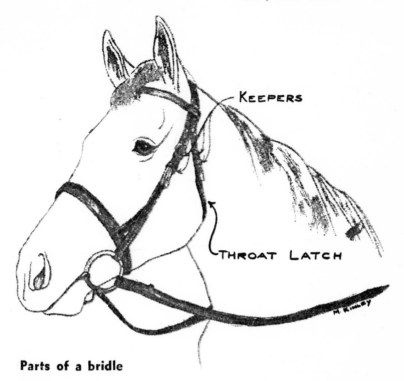

KEEPERS

THROAT LATCH

M. Kinney

Parts of a bridle

you mount (in case your horse bloated and let out his breath when you mounted), and after you have walked your horse for a few minutes. Occasionally, when you are riding, it is wise to check it, too.

3. The throat latch is a safety strap for the bridle which helps prevent the bridle from slipping off the horse's neck.

The keepers keep the ends of straps from flapping and startling your horse.

4. A horse should be led on the left. The rider holds him at the bit with his right hand, while holding the loose ends of the reins in his left hand to prevent them from

dragging on the ground. The reins should be removed from the horse's neck before a horse is led.

5. If a horse stumbles, the rider should keep his balance. He should not fall forward nor jerk on the reins to pull up the horse's head. He should be prepared to make an emergency dismount in case the horse falls down.

4

Blue Ribbon Test

Riding section:

*1. Demonstrate how to take a trot from a walk without jerking on your horse or losing your balance as you begin to post.

*2. Show your ability to post in rhythm during a prolonged trot. (Another horse may trot in front of you.)

3. Turn your horse around and walk in the opposite direction.

4. Make an emergency dismount while your horse is walking.

Horsemanship section:

1. When do you use an emergency dismount?
2. Is it wise to tie a horse by the reins?
3. If you are having trouble leading a horse, what should you do?
4. If, while you are riding, your horse begins to toss his head and prance around, what should you do?
5. What could cause a clicking sound when your horse is trotting?
6. Demonstrate how to tie a horse knot.

Instructor's section:

(To be used with groups of riders)

1. The rider should be willing to ride any horse that is assigned.
2. The rider should be commended for cooperation during class and for consideration for his horse.
3. As an instructor, you should be confident of the rider's safety in a more advanced class.

HOW TO JUDGE YOUR PROFICIENCY ON THE BLUE RIBBON TEST

Riding section:

1. When you ask your horse to trot
   - He should trot immediately when you use leg pressure.
   - *You* should be ready to trot when you ask your horse to trot. Your weight should be forward so you can begin posting almost as soon as he starts trotting.
   - Your reins should be short enough to control your horse, but long enough to prevent you from pulling on his mouth when he trots.

Common mistakes:
   - You should not need to kick your horse. If he is stubborn, you should try to make him go with leg pressure before you use your heels.
   - If he leaps into a trot, you startled him. You should always warn your horse, by picking up your reins and shifting your weight forward a little, that you are going to trot.

- If you fall forward on the neck, or backward on the saddle, or you let your legs swing when you started to post, you were not prepared to trot.
- You should not jerk on the reins.
- You should not use the reins to help you post.

Your transition from a walk to a trot should be smooth. If you cannot keep your balance, if you are unable to begin posting almost at once, or if your horse refuses to trot, you need more practice.

2. You should be able to post in rhythm for five to ten minutes without stopping.
- You should feel relaxed. Posting should seem easy if you are doing it correctly.
- Your elbows should bend as you post.
- Your legs should be as quiet beneath you as when you are walking.
- Your hands should be still.

Common mistakes:
- You should not slip around in the saddle.
- You should not skip a beat nor bounce twice in the same step.
- If your legs swing back and forth, your heels go up and down, or your knees waver in the air, you need to practice posting longer before you go on to the next test.
- You should not catch yourself feeling for the mane.
- Your hands should not ride up and down as you post.
- You should never use your reins for balance.
- You should not look down.
When posting comes to you naturally so you are able to keep your body still except for rising and sitting, when you never need to think of rhythm, when you can trot

for prolonged periods without missing a beat or getting tired, you are ready for intermediate work.

3. When you are turning a horse around
   • You should shorten one rein only *before* you start to turn.
   • You use your leg on the inside of the turn to urge him to turn the direction you have chosen.

Common mistakes:
   • You should not need to kick or tug to turn your horse.
   • You should not jerk on the rein.
   • Your hand should not come way out to the side to turn your horse.
   • Your horse should turn the direction you ask, not the way he decides to go.

This section of the test indicates your ability to ask your horse to work independently in obedience to your commands. Your control over him is what counts. He should do what you ask him to do in the place you ask him to do it.

4. The emergency dismount at a walk should be done in the same way you did it when your horse was standing still. You should walk two or three steps forward after you dismount.

Horsemanship section:

1. The emergency dismount is used if the rider accidentally drops both reins, if the saddle slips to one side, or if an emergency arises when danger is there and the horse refuses to get out of the way. When you are riding and having trouble with your horse, the emergency dismount is used only as a last resort.

2. A horse should not be tied by the reins. He might break his bridle or the reins by pulling away suddenly. The rider will be unable to ride until the bridle is repaired or replaced. A halter and lead rope should be used to tie a horse.

3. If you have trouble leading a horse, stop. Ask for help from the instructor. If you are alone, wait a moment until he is quiet, then try to lead him again. If you are in danger of being hurt, let go of him.

4. If your horse tosses his head and prances in an unusual manner, you may be holding him too tight; loosen the reins. Your horse may be bothered by flies or a bee. He may want to greet another horse or go home. He should be kept under control. Something may be wrong with the way he is saddled, such as a girth that is too tight. Find out what is wrong and correct the trouble.

5. A clicking sound from your horse's hoof is usually caused by a loose shoe. The shoe should be removed.

6. A rider should know how to tie his horse securely. A horse knot can be pulled out easily by a rider but grows tighter when the horse pulls on it. The lead should be just long enough for the horse to touch his nose to the ground. If it is longer, the lead can become twisted around his leg and cut it.

To make a horse knot (See diagram): Wrap the loose

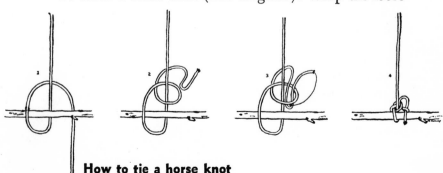

How to tie a horse knot

end of the lead around a tree or strong post. Make a loop around the lead rope with the loose end. Fold the end to make a second loop you can stick through the first one you made. This second loop can be pulled tight to secure the knot, if you have tied it correctly. If the free end of the rope is then pulled through the final loop, it serves as a position "lock" and the knot cannot be untied by a wise horse.

Instructor's section:

1. When you have groups of riders, each one must be willing to ride any one of the horses. This gives your riders the advantages of learning on different mounts and having a variety of riding experiences. You will need to judge a rider more leniently if he is taking a test on a horse that is difficult to ride. It is easier to tell how well a rider has learned to post if he is riding a horse with a gait that does not make posting easy. Be certain you judge the riders, not the horses, when giving tests. A child who controls and stops his horse may well have control only on a horse that is willing to obey. Be sure he has the same control on every horse before he is passed on his Blue Ribbon Test.

The younger a rider is, the more certain you should be of his ability before passing him. This is especially true if he will be competing with older pupils in the more advanced class. At the same time, you must take care not to thwart a rider's progress by keeping him too long with beginners.

2. Your riders need to remember other riders while they are riding. Selfishness can cause accidents as well as unhappiness during class. A rider will never be a horseman unless he learns to treat his horse kindly.

3. The most important qualification for passing a Blue Ribbon Test is security. You want your riders safe in more advanced classes. If their seats are secure, their attitude confident, and their ability up to your standards, they are ready to pass.

Part II

TESTS FOR INTERMEDIATE RIDERS

5
White Ribbon Test

Riding section:

*1. Demonstrate correct form while you trot around the ring.
*2. Demonstrate how to make your horse trot and continue trotting when other horses nearby are not working.
*3. Show how you keep your horse close to the fence and prevent him from cutting corners.
4. Hold double reins correctly.
5. Demonstrate how to make a horse trot
   a. using leg pressure alone
   b. using your heels
   c. using a crop.
6. Give another rider a leg up.

Horsemanship section:

1. Why should a rider prevent his horse from cutting corners?
2. Identify: a. Snaffle b. Pelham c. Curb d. Double or Full Bridle
3. When you ride with a double bridle, which rein is on the outside?

4. Do you ever use the other rein on the outside?
5. Why do you shorten your reins before you ask your horse to trot?

HOW TO JUDGE YOUR PROFICIENCY ON THE WHITE RIBBON TEST

1. Trotting with correct form is important on every test.
 • Your posting should be regular, effortless.
 • You should be sitting up straight, your head erect, your eyes forward, your body relaxed.
 • Your legs and feet should not swing or move when you trot.
 • You must have control of your horse. You gain this control when your hands are sensitive to the movements of the horse's head, when your reins are the correct length—just tight enough for you to feel the bit, but never so tight you use pressure on the bit while you are trotting.

Common mistakes:
 • Your posting should not "go to pieces" because you are in the intermediate group. You should have no double bounces, no sloppy rhythm.
 • Your body should not "melt" in the saddle so that you flop around, slip about, fly with your arms, flap your hands. A neat, controlled body makes for neat, controlled posting.
 • One of the most frequent mistakes intermediate riders make is to let their legs slip forward as soon as they begin to trot. It is worse to let your heels go up.

• If you pull on your reins to keep your balance, or because your reins are too tight, or because you are thinking about something else, your mistake is unforgivable. Your horse should not suffer because you are learning how to ride.

Reins the correct length, hands that feel the horse's mouth—the ideal standard for intermediate riders. Learn to develop gentle hands at the same time that you are learning how to post and how to control your horse. Be sure your wrists are flexible, your hands light against the bit. If you cannot keep from pulling on your horse's mouth, ride with slack reins until you have better balance. You do not need to start posting with your horse's first trotting step, but you should be unshaken if you bounce for a step or two, and your form should be correct.

2. Your horse should trot when other horses are standing still.
    • You need to shorten your reins before you ask him to trot so that he is prepared to trot and so that you have control.
    • You should use leg pressure first to ask him to go, press with your heels if he refuses, and kick as a last resort to make him obey. You may need to keep kicking to keep him trotting.
    • Your weight should be slightly forward as you ask for a trot.

Common mistakes:
    • If you cannot make your horse trot, the most likely reason is because you do not have control. A horse that is allowed to wander in the middle of the ring,

cross the ring, or hurry over to the other horses and stop among them will not trot for you.

• If your heels go up, your seat ceases to be secure. A horse feels your weakness, knows you cannot make him obey, and refuses to trot.

• Your reins should not be tight. A horse will not trot if you are asking him to stop at the same time.

• Your horse should not canter when asked for a trot.

• You should not sit down hard when you post.

Your horse will want to stand still if other horses are standing still. You need to urge him to trot with more persuasion than if the other horses are working at the same time. Your horse should trot steadily around the ring. You will need to use leg pressure even when he is trotting, unless he is a very willing horse. You should be so alert that if he thinks about slowing down you feel his hesitancy and urge him to keep trotting. This section of the test separates intermediates from beginners. You cannot become an adept rider until you can make your horse obey.

3. You should keep your horse close to the fence and prevent him from cutting corners.

• You may only need to use leg pressure with your inside leg on corners.

• You may need slight tension on the outside rein before corners if your horse likes to wander away from the fence.

• You may need to keep the outside rein shorter than the inside rein until your horse learns he cannot have his own way.

• You should use your heels if your horse turns into the center of the ring.

Common mistakes:
- If you do not keep your horse close to the fence all the way around the ring, he will cut the corners.
- If your horse goes into the center of the ring, you must bring him straight back to the fence, or you do not have control.
- If you let your horse cut the corners without correcting him every time, you will not be able to make him stay beside the fence when you trot.

If you cannot keep your horse beside the fence, you should not blame your horse because he is willful and strong. Your inexperience is the cause. Control is the result of coordination in the use of your legs and your hands.

4. You should hold double reins so that the snaffle rein is outside the curb rein. The bight of both reins should lie inside the reins on the right side of your horse's neck.

Common mistakes:
- You should not have twisted reins. The bight should not be twisted.
- You should not allow the curb rein to become tighter than the snaffle once you begin riding.
- Your reins should not be tighter than they are with a snaffle bit alone.

5a. When you make your horse trot with leg pressure
- The calves of your legs should tighten against the horse's sides. The upper part of your leg will press into the saddle.
- You use leg pressure without shifting the position of your legs.

- You should shorten your reins before you begin trotting.
- You should be alert and expecting your horse to trot.

Common mistakes:
- Your leg should not slide back when you use leg pressure.
- You should not lean backward when you are using leg pressure.
- You should not jerk on the reins or raise your hands.

5b. You use your heels to make a horse trot only if leg pressure fails to work.
- You should use pressure with your heel before you resort to a kick.
- If you kick your horse, your heel should strike the horse's side behind the girth with a sharp, hard blow.

Common mistakes:
- You should not kick your horse constantly. You should make him feel the punishment enough so the next time he prefers to trot for leg pressure alone.
- You should not keep your heel up *after* you kick your horse, but should bring your leg back into the correct position for riding.
- You should not jerk on the reins, lean backward, or bounce around in the saddle when you kick your horse.
- Your knee should not go out from the saddle when you kick.
- You should not kick against the girth.

5c. You, as an intermediate rider, should use your crop on your horse's shoulder.
- You should kick your horse at the same time you use the crop.

- You should hold the crop down from your hand, keep your rein in your hand at the same time, and flick your wrist to smack the horse.
- You should use your weight as well as your heels and your crop.

Common mistakes:
- You should not let your crop become tangled in your reins.
- You should not jerk on the reins when you use your crop.
- Your elbow should not fly out as you use your crop.
- The leather loop of your crop should not be over your wrist.

The better you learn to ride, the less you will need to kick to make your horse move faster. However, until you are able to make your horse obey, you need to use everything you can—heels, crop, weight—to force him to do what you want. A sure sign of improved skill is less dependence on your heels and a crop.

6. When giving a rider a leg up, be sure to hold both his ankle and his knee. The rider should cooperate by keeping his upper leg stiff and by jumping up when you ask.

Horsemanship section:

1. A rider proves his control of his horse by preventing him from cutting corners. A horse often refuses to do other things his rider asks if his rider permits him to go where he pleases.

2. (See diagram)

SNAFFLE BIT

a. SNAFFLE: A jointed bit that links in the middle.

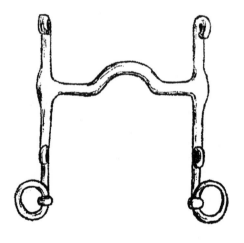

CURB BIT

b. CURB: A bit with a horseshoe-shaped bump in the middle of it.

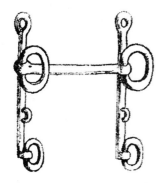 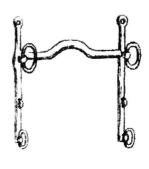

PELHAM BITS

c. PELHAM: May have a straight or curb bit. The shank is long enough and has rings for a double set of reins.

d. FULL BRIDLE: A combination of two bits, a snaffle and a curb, each with a set of reins and headstall.

3. If you have double reins, you ride with your snaffle rein on the outside of your curb rein for normal riding. The snaffle exerts less pressure on the horse's mouth, and does not tighten the curb chain or strap on his chin.

4. If you have trouble controlling your horse you should pick up your curb so that it is tighter than your snaffle. For severe control, you may ride with the curb outside the snaffle.

5. You should shorten your reins before you trot
• to let your horse know you expect something from him.
• so your reins are shorter when you trot. Since the horse tucks his head more at a trot than at a walk, you need shorter reins to have control.

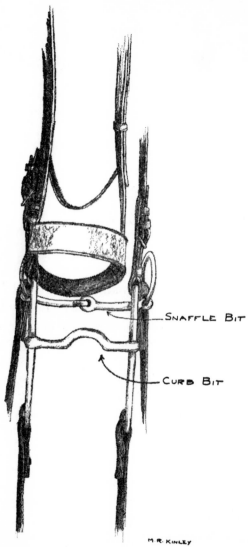

SNAFFLE BIT

CURB BIT

M.R.KINLEY

Full bridle

6

Yellow Ribbon Test

Riding section:

1. Demonstrate the important points to remember when you dismount.
2. Demonstrate the important points to remember when you mount.
3. When you have mounted, show the correct order for adjusting your reins and stirrups. Adjust a stirrup from horseback.
4. Tighten your girth while mounted. Show how to check your girth.
5. Show how a rider, when he is mounting, prevents a horse from
   a. nipping
   b. cow-kicking
   c. backing
6. Turn your horse at a trot using your weight correctly.
7. Circle your horse at a walk.
*8. Trot with slack reins, then shorten your reins and stop your horse correctly.
9. Show how to make a bridge with your reins.

Horsemanship section:

1. Demonstrate how to adjust your stirrups before mounting your horse.

2. Why do you use only one hand to adjust your stirrups from the saddle?

3. What is the purpose of wrapping stirrup leathers? Should you wrap them? Where is the worst place to put your feet?

4. Point out a twisted and untwisted stirrup leather.

5. When do you run up the stirrups on a saddle?

HOW TO JUDGE YOUR PROFICIENCY ON THE YELLOW RIBBON TEST

Riding section:

1. Judge the correct way to dismount by checking the following points:

 • Both reins are in your left hand. Your left hand is on your horse's mane.

 • The bight of the reins is shifted to the left side of your horse's neck.

 • Your right hand is in the hollow of the saddle above the right stirrup leather.

 • Your weight is so well balanced, as your right leg is swinging over your horse's back, that you can swing it back and forth without shifting your weight or moving the rest of your body.

 • Your elbows are straight, your weight balanced easily on your hands, as you take your left foot out of the stirrup. You are able to hold this position so well you can

put your foot in the stirrup again without difficulty.
• When you drop lightly to the ground, you slide down
with your side against the horse so you land facing the
front of your horse.
• You take the reins at the bit with your right hand.
If you are preparing to leave the ring, you take the
reins off your horse's neck and hold the ends of the
reins in your left hand. You finish the dismount standing
at the side of your horse's head.

Common mistakes:
• If you forget to shift the bight of the reins to the left
side, it will drag across the horse's withers while you are
dismounting.
• You should not shift your right hand to the back of
the saddle, nor put your left hand on the front of the
saddle, in the middle of the dismount.
• You should not touch your horse with your leg or heel
while dismounting.
• Your right knee should not bend through the saddle.
• You should not lose your balance and fall against
your horse or drop to the ground with one foot still in
the stirrup.
• The left stirrup should not bang your horse's side
because you dismounted too quickly and kicked your
foot out of the stirrup as you flew off the horse.
• You should not lean on the saddle with your stomach,
or slide off your horse on your stomach.
• You should not land with a thump on the ground.
• When you shift your right hand from the saddle to
the reins at the bit, you should not let go of the reins
with your left hand until you have a firm hold on them
with your right.

• You should fail this section if you drop your reins while you are dismounting.

2. Judge the correct way to mount by checking the following points:
  • You should check your girth before you mount.
  • You should lengthen your stirrup if you cannot reach it with your foot.
  • Both reins and some of the mane should be held in your left hand.
  • Your right hand rests across the pommel of the saddle.
  • The bight of the reins should be on the left side of the neck.
  • You should be balanced as you swing onto your horse, and sit down lightly in the saddle.
  • The bight of the reins should be shifted to the right side.

Common mistakes:
  • You should not kick your horse nor jerk on his mouth when you mount.
  • You should be so well balanced that you do not yank the saddle off your horse's back.
  • Your left stirrup should not be so long that you can barely get your leg across your horse's croup.

Each detail of dismounting and mounting should be so natural to you that you can mount correctly without giving thought to how you do it.

3. Your reins should be adjusted before you adjust your stirrups. Control is more important than having your stirrups the correct length.

To adjust your stirrups from horseback:
  • You should pull the buckle down from the saddle so that you can see it and unfasten it.
  • Using only your left hand to adjust your left stirrup, pull on the stirrup to shorten it, and push with your foot to lengthen it.
  • Do not let go of the reins while adjusting your stirrup.
  • You should not leave the buckle exposed. Run it back up close to the saddle by pushing on the stirrup with your foot while lifting the strap with your hand to give it slack.
  • One of your stirrups should not be longer than the other.
4. When you tighten your girth from horseback
  • You lift the skirt of the saddle, pull up on one billet, then the other, until the girth is tight.
  • You should be able to put four fingers under the girth.

Common mistakes:
  • You should not drop the reins or let go of the mane while you are concentrating on tightening your girth.
  • One billet should not be tighter than the other.
  • Be careful not to get the girth too tight.

The most common mistake riders make when tightening girths is to use two hands for the billets and none for the reins. You can feel what you are doing and do not need to see if both billets are even until you make a final check.

5. A horse can be prevented from displaying bad habits when a rider is mounting.
  a. If a horse tends to nip, the rider can tighten the rein on the off-side to prevent the horse from turning his head around.

b. If a horse tries to cow-kick, he cannot kick the rider who mounts facing the rear of his horse. A good swat with the crop on the leg, or a sharp kick as the foot comes off the ground, does a good job of discouraging cow-kicking.

c. If a horse backs up when the rider is mounting, the rider may be pulling on the reins. If the horse backs although the reins are loose, the rider can mount in a corner of the ring with the horse's rump touching the fence.

6. In order to turn your horse correctly at a trot
 • You should look in the direction you are turning, thereby shifting your weight to indicate the turn to the horse.
 • Your rein on the inside of the turn should be shorter than the other rein. The less pressure you need to put on this rein to turn, the better.
 • You should use leg pressure on the inside of the turn.
 • You should have enough room to turn for your horse to be able to trot without stopping.
 • You should not pull on the outside rein.
 • You indicate you cannot control your horse correctly if your horse does not turn *when* you ask him or *where* you ask him.
 • If it takes you the entire ring to make your horse turn, you are not using your hands, legs and weight correctly.
 • The bit should not be pulled out of the horse's mouth on one side.
 • The horse should not just turn his head without turning his body to go where you want.
 • Your horse should not stop trotting half-way around the turn.

Your horse should turn quietly, without fighting your light control. You should be looking in the direction you are going all the time you are turning.

7. When you circle your horse at a walk, you use only one rein, the inside leg, and the shift of weight caused by looking where you are going, just as you did when you turned. You should have enough room to make a round circle as small as it is possible for your horse to make easily.

8. You should be able to trot with slack reins.
   • Your horse should keep at a steady trot. You should not need to check him frequently with the reins.
   • Your posting should be smooth, your position upright.

When you shorten your reins before stopping
   • You should pick up your reins until you have contact with the horse's mouth without pulling on the reins or shifting your hands noticeably.
   • Your posting should continue smoothly while you are shortening the reins.

When you stop your horse
   • Your weight should be shifted backwards by lifting your head.
   • When you pull on the reins, they should already be short enough so that you need only a short pull to make your horse stop.
   • Your weight should push into your heels.
   • You should post until you are ready to stop, then sit into the saddle.
   • Your horse should make a complete stop within a few steps.

Common mistakes:
- Your hands should not move up and down as you trot with slack reins.
- Your elbows should not flop in and out as you post.
- You should not need to lean forward in order to post when your reins are slack.
- Your horse should not trot too fast.
- He should not cut corners, or go into the center of the ring, or come too close to other horses when you are trotting with slack reins.
- Your posting should not become uneven as you pick up your reins or check your horse to prevent him from cutting corners.
- You should be able to shorten your reins without jerking on your horse.
- Your reins should not be too long when you stop your horse so that your hands go out to the side or come back over the middle of the saddle.
- You should not forget to release the pressure on the reins as soon as your horse stops.
- You should not look down while you are shortening your reins or stopping.
- You should not let your horse stop trotting until you ask him to stop.

It takes balance to post evenly with slack reins. This section tests your ability to maintain that balance when you are thinking about control of your horse, shortening your reins, staying away from other horses without making a sudden jerk on one rein. It also tests your ability to keep your horse trotting and to stop correctly. Many riders begin to arch their backs to post when their reins are slack. When they try to stop, they lose the rhythm of posting, or depend on the reins more than their weight to stop the horse. You need to do every part of this section correctly in order to pass.

9. When you make a bridge with your reins, the right rein crosses into your left hand and your left rein passes through your right hand so that you are holding both reins with both hands. The short section of doubled-up reins between your hands is a "bridge."

Horsemanship section:

1. In order to adjust your stirrups from the ground
   • You lower the buckle until you can reach it easily.
   • The stirrup is measured from your armpit to your thumb or third finger. You should know whether your stirrup is the correct length when you touch your thumb or your third finger to the top of the leather.
   • Remember to run the buckle into place again.
2. When you adjust your stirrups in the saddle, you use only one hand for the adjustment so you have control of your horse with the reins in the other hand.
3. You may need to wrap the leathers around the stirrups if your legs are short, because the leathers will not go short enough. It is better if you punch new holes at even intervals than to wrap your stirrup leathers. The worst place to put your feet is inside the leathers because they will not slip out easily if your horse stumbles and falls.
4. A twisted stirrup leather cuts edgewise into a rider's leg. An untwisted stirrup leather rests flat along the rider's leg or boot.
5. Stirrups should be run to the top of the leathers when you dismount and when you store your saddle.

To run up the stirrups, you lift the stirrup up the back of the leathers, then tuck the leathers through the stirrup to the back side.

7

Red Ribbon Test

Riding section:

1. Trot around the ring without using your stirrups. (A lead horse may be used.)
*2. Circle your horse at a trot.
3. Circle your horse in a group of horses which are also circling.
*4. Trot down the side of the ring on the correct diagonal. Make a reverse by turning out from the fence at a 45 degree angle and reversing toward the fence. Trot in the opposite direction on the correct diagonal.
*5. Demonstrate a good seat at a trot.
*6. Quiet hands demonstrated throughout the test.
    a. Reins the correct length.
    b. Angle and placement of your hands correct.

Horsemanship section:

1. Why should you know how to post on different diagonals?
2. Explain the importance of good hands and seat.
3. Explain two important safety rules when riding in a group.

4. Demonstrate the correct way to lead a horse.
5. Lead a stubborn horse.
6. Show how to lead an eager horse.
7. Why do you avoid facing your horse when you are leading him?
8. Check the bridle on your horse.
9. Check the saddle on your horse.

HOW TO JUDGE YOUR PROFICIENCY
ON THE RED RIBBON TEST

Riding section:

1. When you trot without stirrups
   • Keep your horse trotting slowly to help you sit to his trot.
   • Your horse should trot at a steady pace.
   • You should be relaxed as you trot.
   • Your legs should hang naturally at the horse's sides.

Common mistakes:
   • You should not use the reins for balance because this makes you pull on your horse's mouth.
   • You should not slip back and forth in the saddle.
   • Your toes should not stick up in the air or out to the sides at right angles to your horse.
   • If you are tense and tight, you will bounce more.

You should have a sense of balance when you trot without stirrups. Sometimes when you are riding for pleasure, you will not want to use your stirrups, and you should begin to feel comfortable without them. The secret is trotting slowly. This exercise also helps you learn to sit to a slow trot.

2. When you circle your horse at a trot
   • He should trot at a steady pace without stopping or slowing down.
   • You should trot in a round circle.
   • The circle should be small enough to be recognized as a circle.
   • You should look where you are going so that you shift your weight to the inside of the circle.

Common mistakes:
   • You should not end up going in the opposite direction.
   • Your horse should not tug you toward the fence or the center of the ring so that your circle is oblong or straight on one side.
   • Your hands should be still, your horse under control, as you circle so that you do not need to pull suddenly or jerk on your horse's mouth to turn him in the right direction.

The most common mistake riders make when circling their horses is not allowing enough room for the circle so their horses have to stop trotting in the middle of the circle. This exercise is judged mainly on control. You should use your hands lightly. Your legs ask for the turn but also keep your horse trotting.

3. When you circle your horse at the same time other riders are circling their horses, you need to use the same control as if you were alone. In addition, you have to

watch where the other riders are going and make sure your horse does not collide with another horse or have to stop trotting because there is not enough room.

4. To trot on the correct diagonal
   • You should be out of the saddle, at the top of your posting, when your horse's foreleg closest to the fence is as far forward as he steps.

To reverse (one method of reverse you should know.)
   • Your horse should trot away from the fence at a 45-degree angle. He begins to reverse toward the fence while he is still trotting in the same direction, but as he reaches the fence he turns in the opposite direction.
   • You should look in the direction you are going.

Common mistakes:
   • You should not be posting on the wrong diagonal, nor forget to change diagonals when you change directions.
   • You should not finish a reverse going in the same direction as before.
   • Your horse should not stop trotting, nor should he change his pace.
   • You should not lose your balance, or your posting rhythm.
   • You should not jerk on the reins or let your hands fly in the air.

To reverse correctly, you should reverse smoothly, using your hands for guidance, your head to shift your weight, and your inside leg to help your horse turn. Your change of diagonals should be almost unnoticeable. You may also reverse by turning around toward the inside of the ring (see diagram).

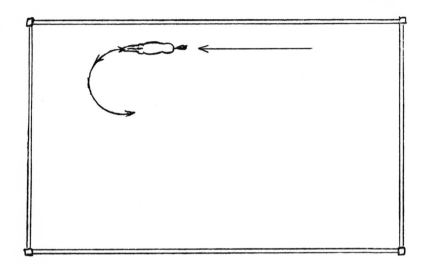

REVERSE

5. Your position should be more secure at a trot now than when you took the White Ribbon Test.

• Your legs should be directly under you, your heels down. Your muscles should be firm enough, the position natural enough to you, so that there is no tension in your legs. This means your heels stay down as you post. The horse never feels your heels touch his sides unless you want him to feel them.

• You post close to the saddle—smoothly, easily.

• You feel relaxed, although your body is straight, your eyes always forward, your hands and legs quiet.

Common mistakes:

• If your knees are not bent slightly as you post, you will either post too high, or your legs will swing forward. Your legs should not straighten out completely at the top of your posting.

• An observer, looking at you from behind, should not see six or seven inches of daylight between you and the saddle. He should not see daylight between your knees and your horse.

By the time you take this test, you should have proper form all the time you are trotting and control of your horse as well. You should keep your balance when you start and stop, when you turn and circle.

6. Quiet hands mean:

• Only when you give a signal to your horse do you move your hands. Your hands should be steady, firm, and move decisively when you give a signal to your horse.

• Your hands are resilient, soft on the reins, easy on

your horse's mouth. If your horse bobs his head back and forth, your hands should yield to him, rather than having the reins go slack and then tight at each step.

• You should feel your horse's mouth in your hands so that even a small pull with your fingers puts tension on the reins.

• The backs of your hands should have the same slant as your horse's withers. Your hands are a few inches apart, one on each side of his neck, and do not cross over to the opposite side to turn. They should be in a position that is comfortable for the rider. The thicker the horse's neck, the further apart your hands should be.

• When you shorten your reins, your hands move gently.

• Your elbows bend and straighten as you post.

Common mistakes:

• You should not flip your reins up in the air to shift the bight to the other side of the neck or to straighten out the reins.

• Your hands should not move up and down as you post, as you turn, or as you pull on the reins.

• Your reins should not be tight. You should not snatch at your horse's mouth.

• Your reins should not be uneven—one rein longer than the other.

• Your reins should not be twisted. The bight should not be on the left side while you are riding. The ends of the reins should not stick up through your fists.

• Your elbows should not be out because this causes your hands to turn inward out of place.

• Your wrists should not be "cocked" so your palms are

facing the horse's neck. Your wrists should not be rigid. You should not make fists of your hands.

Horsemanship sections:

1. You need to know diagonals if you plan to ride in shows. You need to know how to change diagonals so that you do not always post on the same one when you ride your horse. If you do not change diagonals, your horse's muscles can become overdeveloped on one side.
2. You want to have good hands in order to give your horse signals in the way he understands. You need a good seat so that you are balanced properly in the saddle and can use your weight and your legs correctly to guide your horse.
3. Some of the important safety rules for riding are:
   • When you ride behind another horse, you should be far enough away to see his heels when you look between your horse's ears.
   • You should leave room for another rider to pass if you are riding in a ring.
   • Courtesy is safety. Let the other horse go first. Take turns. Do not barge ahead of other horses. If someone is having trouble with a horse, keep out of the way.
   • Never yell, throw things, make sudden movements, or play jokes around horses.
   • Do not blame another rider for his mistakes with his horse. Watch your own horse instead.
4. You should lead a horse on his left. He is held at the bit with your right hand; the loose ends of the reins are in your left hand.
5. A stubborn horse can usually be encouraged to walk if you lead him first to one side, then the other, until he

takes a step. After he walks to the side, he will usually walk forward. Do not hit him on the rump, or let anyone else hit him, because he might kick.

6. An eager horse can be turned in circles until you are able to bring him under control. If you push your elbow against his shoulder, you keep yourself away from his feet and have some leverage to pull on the lead.

7. You avoid facing a horse when you are trying to lead him because he usually refuses to go when you are looking at him.

8. When you check your bridle:
  • Are the keepers fastened?
  • Is the throat latch fastened? Is it loose so that your hand slides under it with ample room?
  • Is the curb untwisted and flat? Can you slip your fingers under it? Does it tighten against the horse's chin when you put tension on the curb rein?
  • Does the bit rest comfortably in the horse's mouth or does he mouth it and toss his head constantly?

9. When you check your saddle:
  • Is the saddle pad directly under the saddle and forward enough to protect the horse's withers?
  • Is the saddle well forward over the withers?
  • If the girth is a leather one, is it on frontwards? The fold should be toward the horse's forelegs.
  • Is the girth just tight enough so that you can get four fingers under it?
  • Is the girth the same number of holes up on each side (or only one hold tighter on one side than the other)?

8

Blue Ribbon Test

Riding Section:

1. While you are trotting, change diagonals every ten steps. Demonstrate good hands and seat at the same time.
*2. Demonstrate how to post so close to the saddle that there is little daylight visible between you and your horse as you post. Show how to keep your hands and arms in the correct position.
3. Back your horse using your hands, legs and weight correctly.
*4. Demonstrate a prolonged trot at a steady gait.
5. Trot three minutes without stirrups.
6. Demonstrate how to walk, turn and stop a horse when you are riding bareback.
7. Trot a serpentine.
8. Demonstrate a change of direction using the entire ring.

Horsemanship section:

1. A horse is measured in ———s, each of which equals

———— inches. They are measured from ———— to ————.

2. The average height of a horse is ————.
3. A pony is less than ———— in height.
4. What is the average life span of a horse?
5. A horse ———— years old is considered aged.
6. Which is the near side of a horse? What is the other side called?
7. Describe: palomino, pinto, chestnut, bay.
8. What are the distinctive characteristics of: Arab, Morgan, Thoroughbred, Saddlebred.

Instructor's section:

(*This part of the test is used only where groups of riders are taught.*)
1. The rider should help in the stable area for a minimum of an hour.
2. The rider should help put horses in their stalls after a riding period.
3. A younger rider or beginner should be assisted in leading a horse.
4. The rider should show how to tie a horse, and turn him loose.
5. The rider should be commended for cooperation and a willing attitude.
6. During class hours, the rider should be willing to ride any horse assigned to him.
7. He should be able to keep his distance when riding with other horses.
8. A rider should know how to saddle and bridle his horse before passing into the advanced ring.

HOW TO JUDGE YOUR PROFICIENCY
ON THE BLUE RIBBON TEST

Riding section:

1. To change diagonals every ten steps:
   • You need good balance as you sit or stand the extra beat to make the change.
   • Your hands should be still while you change diagonals.
   • Your legs should be still while you change diagonals.

Common mistakes:
   • You should not need to shift your weight way forward while you are changing diagonals.
   • You should not pull on the reins as you change diagonals, either to catch your balance or because you bounce.
   • You should not forget to change diagonals or miss changing on the tenth step.
   • If your hands jerk on the reins or your legs swing, you are unbalanced.

This is an exercise for balance and a good seat. It is important your hands do not emphasize what you are doing with your body when you sit a beat or stand a beat to change diagonals.

2. In order to post close to the saddle:
   • Your thighs should stay close to the saddle.
   • Your knees do not straighten very far.

- You post only as high as necessary to avoid bouncing.
- Your arms remain close to your sides.
- Your hands remain steady and still in front of the saddle. They seem to be independent of your body movement.

Common mistakes:

- You might find yourself bouncing a bit in the saddle because you are posting too close to the saddle. Sometimes you *want* to bounce in order to make sure you are posting low enough.
- You should not be rising more than three or four inches off the saddle on horses with an easy gait or on ponies. If a horse has a rough trot, you will need to post slightly higher.
- You should not find it difficult to balance when you post close to the saddle—you should not be using the reins or the mane to post; you should neither be arching excessively nor leaning forward.

It takes practice and concentration to post close to the saddle. The important part of the test is to be posting lower than you did as a beginner. You should be feeling the horse push you out of the saddle, instead of thinking of standing up and sitting down by straightening and bending your knees as you stand on the stirrups. Posting should appear effortless because you are no longer working at it.

3. When you back your horse correctly:
- Your head should be raised so it is slightly back in order to put your weight back in the saddle.

- When you pull on the reins, use just enough tension so the horse backs willingly.
- You use leg pressure equally on both sides of your horse.

Common mistakes:
- Do not look down. This shifts your weight forward.
- Do not let your heels come up or you lose your balance and shift your weight forward.
- Your reins should not be uneven or the horse will back crookedly.
- You should not press harder with one leg or your horse will back unevenly.

4. In a prolonged trot:
- Your horse should move freely at a steady pace.
- You should use leg pressure as you post if he begins to slow down.
- You should check him with the reins if he trots too fast.
- He should trot beside the fence, into the corners, and pass other horses without slowing down or trying to move in among them.

Common mistakes:
- Your horse should not stop of his own accord.
- You should not use leg pressure, or kick him, at the same time you pull on the reins. You should not kick him if he is moving along steadily.
- He should not canter.
- He should not alternately slow down, then trot more quickly.

• He should not trot where he wants, but where you want to go.

You should be able to trot for several minutes steadily without tiring. Your horse should move willingly with a minimum of leg pressure and guidance.

5. When you trot without stirrups:
   • Your horse stays in a slow, controlled trot.
   • Your legs should hang down with your toes dropped.
   • Your seat should be secure, your hands still.
   • You should be relaxed.

Common mistakes:
   • You should not let your hands ride up and down as you bounce.
   • You should not be bouncing gaily and thumping your horse's back.
   • Your reins should not be tight, only short enough to check your horse to keep him trotting slowly.
   • You should be sitting erect, not leaning forward.

You may find it a bit difficult to sit without stirrups. If you bounce a lot, you are not relaxed, and are likely to jerk on the reins as you bounce. The one mistake you should not make is to pull on the horse's mouth because you cannot keep your hands still, or because you cannot keep your balance.

6. When you walk bareback:
   • Your position should be the same as when you ride with a saddle, except your legs dangle at your horse's sides with your toes down.

• When you turn, you should keep your head up and look where you are going, use leg pressure on the inside, and tighten the inside rein.

• When you stop, you use your weight and hands in the same way you do if you have a saddle.

Common mistakes:

• You should not slip off at a walk.

• You should not use your reins for balance, although you may hold the mane.

• You should not move carelessly, look the wrong way, or pull your horse about roughly, as if he were a toy.

Bareback riding helps you feel the movement of your horse so that you are able to move with him, and it improves your balance. You should appear at ease as you walk your horse.

7. When you trot a serpentine (see diagram):

• Your half circles should have parallel sides.

• You should change diagonals as you cross the center of the ring.

• Your horse should trot at a steady pace.

Common mistakes:

• You should not post on the wrong diagonal.

• You should not be trotting in vague loops, but in a precise pattern.

8. When you change direction using the entire ring:

• You should begin to cross the ring diagonally when you are a third of the way down one side.

• You cross the ring to a point a third of the way from

Serpentine

Start your serpentine at the center of a side at A or C. Change diagonals at the Xs. Stop your serpentine at the center of the ring at A or C.

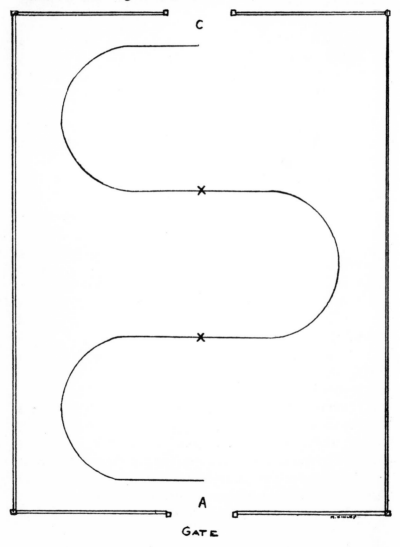

the far end of the ring and continue trotting in the same direction.
- As you come around the ring, you will be trotting the opposite way.

Common mistakes:
- You should not finish the figure trotting in the same direction as you began.
- If your horse does not cross when you want, or trot where you want, you lack control.
- Your horse should not stop trotting.

Horsemanship section:

1. A horse is measured in hands, each of which equals four inches. They are measured from the horse's withers to the ground.
2. The average height of a horse is 16 to 17 hands.
3. A pony is 14 hands and 2 inches, or less.
4. The average life span of a horse is 23 to 25 years.
5. A horse is considered aged at 9.
6. The near side of a horse is the left side. The other side is called the off side.
7. PALOMINO: He has a pale golden color with a flaxen mane and tail.
   PINTO: He is a spotted horse.
   CHESTNUT: He has a brown muzzle and either a cream or brown mane and tail. His color is redder than a bay's.
   BAY: He has a black mane, tail and muzzle.
8. An Arabian is a small horse, higher at the croup than at the withers. He has a finely-shaped head, dished face and small ears. He is known for his endurance.
   A Morgan is a compact horse with smooth lines, stylish

action, a crested neck and small ears. His back is shorter than a Thoroughbred's. He is an easy-keeper and is known for his endurance and gentleness. His disposition is good because he does not tend to be nervous.

A Thoroughbred has thin skin, small head and ears, a long slender neck and a fineness of line. He does not carry his head high. Speed is the quality most often associated with a Thoroughbred. Thoroughbreds tend to be sensitive horses.

The Saddlebred's back is longer and his hind quarters higher than a Thoroughbred's. When he trots, the Saddlebred spreads his hind legs wide apart and puts them down ahead of and outside the prints made by his forelegs. He takes long strides.

Instructor's section:

1. The greatest asset when you are teaching group riding is to have willing helpers. If you can encourage your riders to help as part of the daily routine, the groups you teach will be happier. However, if your riders tend to be reluctant helpers, you will need to emphasize this part of the test as part of their training with horses. No one should ride horses without understanding something about their care and needs. This help can include walking horses after classes, putting horses in their stalls, untacking, cleaning tack, or simply putting hay in the stalls. If you have a large number of eager helpers, you may need to outline the duties you want done the most as part of this test, such as cleaning stalls.

2. A rider should know how to lead a horse into a stall and put on a halter. At the end of a class, your riders

should take their own horses into the stable as part of the routine.

3. Riders should learn early the benefits of helping less experienced or beginning riders. It is a great asset to an instructor to have more experienced riders willing to lead horses of the beginners who are learning how. You need to watch the attitude of the helpers, however, to be sure the beginners are not discouraged by them.

4. All of your helpers should know how long to tie a rope on a horse. They should know how to move out of a box stall after turning a horse loose inside, so that they are not stepped on and do not let the horse out behind them. If your horses are turned out to pasture, your riders should learn to turn them to face the gate before releasing them in order to have time to move away before the horses kick up their heels.

5. Every rider should cooperate with the instructors. A rider who rushes from a lesson without a care about what happens to his horse misses his chance to know his horse as an individual. An understanding of his horse enables him to ride more intelligently. A superior or belligerent attitude toward assistant instructors deprives a rider of gaining from the knowledge each instructor has.

6. When different people will be riding your horses, everyone must accept your decisions about which horse to ride. You cannot afford hard feelings among your riders when one member of the class refuses to ride one of the horses. Such a refusal also prevents that rider from gaining the advantages of new skills you want him to have from riding that horse.

7. Any rider who continuously forgets to keep his distance should not be passed into the advanced ring. Once there,

where he is not watched as carefully, he could cause an accident. Where safety is concerned, rules come before riders.

8. A rider should not consider himself advanced if he cannot saddle and bridle, and unsaddle and unbridle, a horse.

Part III

TESTS FOR ADVANCED RIDERS

9

White Ribbon Test

Riding section:

1. Trot, stop and reverse bareback.
*2. Demonstrate how to sit your horse at a canter.
3. Show the correct way to make an unwilling horse canter.
4. Point out a horse on the correct lead; one on the incorrect lead.
*5. Demonstrate good hands and seat while you trot, reverse and ride in the opposite direction past a line of horses.
6. Circle at a trot.

Horsemanship section:

1. Locate the parts of a horse.
2. When is it safe to give a horse a friendly swat on the croup?
3. As long as you are not inside the riding ring where riders are mounted is it safe to shout and race through the stable area?
4. What are the safety rules involving: bare feet, remov-

ing a jacket in the riding ring, hard hats, smoking in the stable area, working around a horse or underneath him?

HOW TO JUDGE YOUR PROFICIENCY ON THE WHITE RIBBON TEST

Riding section:

1. When you are riding bareback, check the following points:
   • You should sit in a relaxed position, your elbows in, your legs hanging down with your toes dropped, your shoulders up, your eyes forward.
   • You should not bounce excessively when you trot. Your horse should stay in a slow trot. You should not need to catch the mane for balance.
   • When you stop, you remember to shorten the reins and are able to stop your horse quickly. You do not need to hold the mane to keep from falling off.
   • When you reverse, you use your hands correctly, you use leg pressure on the inside of a turn, you keep your balance, and you are able to make your horse go where you ask.

Common mistakes:
   • Your shoulders should not be hunched forward, a sign of a tense body.
   • Your reins should not be so tight your horse's chin is tucked. This is a sign of a lack of confidence in your ability to control your horse.
   • You should not need to hold the mane, but a worse fault is tugging on the reins.
   • You should not slide off.

When you are riding bareback, you should have as good control as when you ride with a saddle. Only your fear of slipping off, which makes you tense, prevents you from having control. If you let your horse trot too fast, your bouncing may interfere with your control.

2. At a canter:
   • You are relaxed so that your muscles give to the movement of the horse.
   • You sit up straight and your body is still. You are looking forward.
   • Your reins are short enough to give you control of your horse, but you are not depending on them for balance.
   • You are able to make your horse canter when you ask.

Common mistakes:
   • Your body should not be so tense you are jarred by every step.
   • Your shoulders should not pump forward and backward.
   • You should not jerk on the reins while you are cantering or when you stop.
   • You should be able to stop your horse within ten steps, rather than letting him canter some distance before he stops.

The major criterion for passing this test is sitting your canter. You should practice until you feel at ease cantering and do not bounce much. You should demonstrate control by being able to canter your horse when you want and stop when you want.

3. If a horse is unwilling to canter,
   - You should use your hands and your feet together, with leg pressure or a kick on the outside, and lifting with the inside rein (unless your horse is trained to canter with a lift on the outside rein).
   - You are able to kick effectively if needed until your horse responds with a canter.
   - You are able to use your crop effectively with your heels.
   - You use your weight correctly, shifting it forward as you ask for the canter.
   - You are able to make him canter where you want in the ring.

Common mistakes:
   - If your horse will not canter, you may not have enough control to keep him close to the fence. This makes him refuse to do what you ask.
   - You should not have your reins tight.
   - You should not have the rein you use to ask for the canter tight all the time.
   - You should not jerk on the reins.
   - You should not kick continuously without results.
   - You should not be leaning back.

Once you are able to make a willing horse canter and sit his canter, you need to know how to make any horse canter. This is the best way to test your skill in using the right aids to ask for a canter.

4. A horse on the correct lead will canter so that his foreleg toward the inside of the ring goes further forward

than the foreleg toward the fence. A horse on the wrong lead will reach further forward with his outside foreleg.

You need to recognize leads when other horses are cantering before you will be able to tell with your own horse. It is easier to tell leads if you see a horse from the side than if you look down at his forelegs from the saddle.

5. Both control and position need to be good when you trot past a line of horses going in the opposite direction from you.

Control:
• You should respond to any tendency on your horse's part to change his direction without your consent. You should be decisive, immediate and steady with your corrections.
• Your horse should obey.
• Your horse should be so conscious of your control by the time you have reversed to face the other horses that he trots willingly past them.
• He should trot at a steady pace without the need for constant urging from you.
• He should trot close enough to the other horses to let you touch an outstretched arm, but should pass without paying attention to the other horses.

Position:
• Your hands should be low, quiet, and steady, moving only to correct your horse.
• You should be posting on the correct diagonal before and after reversing.
• Your heels should be down.

Common mistakes:

Control:
- If you cannot make your horse trot, if you cannot keep him trotting at a steady pace, or if he refuses to face the other horses, you do not have control.
- If he is belligerent or tries to barge in among the other horses, you should not fail to punish him.
- You should not let him turn around of his own accord.
- You should not need to kick him all the time he is trotting in order to make him obey.

Position:
- You should not jerk on your reins, let your hands fly high, or let your reins get too long.
- You should not waver off a straight line or look like a scarecrow while you are passing the other horses.
- Your legs should not flop away from your horse's sides.
- You should not hunch forward while you are trying to control your horse.
- You should not lose your temper or get upset because your horse refuses to obey.

A test of your ability to control your horse at a trot is to have him work in opposition to other horses. You need to be able to work your horse independently. Your position should not suffer because you have trouble with your horse, or because you are thinking about controlling him.

6. When you circle your horse at a trot:
- You should be able to make round circles, oblong circles, flat circles, at will.

- You should be able to trot without changing your pace or interfering with other horses who are also working in the ring.
- You should be posting on the correct diagonal.

Common mistakes:

- You should not be forced to stop because you did not allow enough room for your horse to trot.
- You should not forget how to use your weight or your legs. You should not need to tug on the inside rein. Slight pressure on a rein should give results.
- You should not trot in such a small circle your horse cannot trot easily.

Horsemanship section:

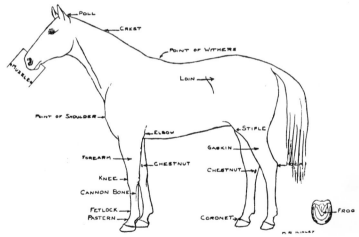

Parts of the horse

1. (See diagram)

PASTERN: Indented joint on the horse's leg just above the hoof.

FETLOCKS: Joint on the horse's leg above the pastern

which has long hair (called the "feathers") on the back side of it.

CANNON BONE: The long bone in the horse's legs between his fetlocks and knees in front, between his fetlocks and hocks behind.

KNEE: The joint that bends forward in the middle of his forelegs.

HOCK: The large bone that bends backward in the middle of his hind legs.

STIFLE: The flabby part at the top of his hind legs.

CORONET: The tiny ridge around the top of his hoof.

CHESTNUT: The hard callouses that look as if they were blemishes on the inside of his legs.

POLL: The bump between a horse's ears.

CREST: The ridge of a horse's neck.

FROG: Center section like a V inside a horse's hoof.

POINT OF SHOULDER: The front of the bone that presses forward under the skin of his shoulder. You can feel it as you back your horse.

POINT OF WITHERS: The highest part of the withers.

LOINS: The indented area on the horse's side behind where the saddle rests.

FOREARM: The upper half of a horse's front leg.

ELBOW: The joint that bends (as a human elbow bends) at the top of a horse's forelegs.

MUZZLE: The projecting part of a horse's head including the mouth, nose and jaws.

GASKIN: The upper part of the hind leg of a horse.

2. Never swat a horse on the croup. If you want to move a horse to one side of his stall, speak to him first, then push against his rump to ask him to step to the side. (Be sure you are close enough not to be hurt if he kicks.)

3. Horses have sensitive ears which makes it dangerous

to shout in the stable area. You may not be in danger, but some other rider may be. If you race around in the stable area, you catch the attention of the horses, and, since they do not like sudden movements, this could be dangerous.

4. Some of the safety rules to obey around horses include:
- Do not go barefoot.
- If you must remove a jacket while you are riding, dismount to take it off. Do not drop it or toss it aside. Put it where it will not flap in the wind or fall to the ground in the path of a horse.
- A hard hat is protection for you. Wear one when you jump. It is wise to wear one on trail. Many instructors prefer to have you wear one whenever you ride.
- Do not smoke in a stable area.
- Move quietly and with assurance around horses. Never go under a horse's stomach or neck. He may not intend to kick you, but you may be in the way when he kicks at a fly.

10
Trail Test

A rider should pass this test before going alone on a trail ride.

1. Stop at command from a walk, a trot, a canter.
2. Show several ways to stop a runaway horse.
3. Demonstrate a relaxed seat at a walk, a trot, a canter.
4. Explain the use of leads and diagonals on trail.
5. Make an emergency dismount at a trot.
6. Circle at a canter.
7. Explain safety rules for trail rides including: bareback riding, distance from other horses, crossing streets, crossing water, riding double, how to help another rider in trouble, how to go through bushes when another horse is behind you, how to canter around curves.

Whenever possible you should ride with someone else when you go on a trail ride. This test gives you a standard to judge whether you will be safe on trail.

Remember that there are few barriers on a trail to help stop your horse once you have lost control of him. You should not go out alone on trail until you have control of your horse at a canter.

HOW TO JUDGE WHETHER IT IS SAFE FOR YOU
TO TAKE A TRAIL RIDE

1. Your horse should stop immediately when you want, at the exact place you want, no matter what gait he is in. If you cannot stop within a few steps after you ask your horse to stop, or if you cannot keep your horse standing still after he stops, do not go on trail.

2. You may stop a runaway horse
   • By seesawing back and forth on the reins.
   • By turning your horse in circles so that each circle is smaller than the previous one until he is forced to slow down.
   • By bracing one hand against his neck and jerking with sharp hard tugs on the reins in your other hand. (Do not demonstrate how to jerk on your horse's mouth. You jerk on it only in emergencies.)

Remember the most important thing to do if your horse gets out of control is to keep calm. Guide him so that he does not scrape you on trees or run through someone's rose garden. If you keep your head, you will be able to stay on and stop him.

3. A relaxed seat at any gait means
   • You feel comfortable and at ease in the saddle.
   • You look confident because you are confident.
   • Your elbows are at your sides, your hands and wrists flexible.
   • Your legs stay in position without strain. Your heels stay down without an effort on your part.

Common mistakes:

- Your shoulders should not be hunched forward. You should not lean forward apprehensively as if you expected trouble.
- You should not feel as if you wanted to grab the mane for support.
- You should not be tense so that you cannot easily flex your wrists, elbows, knees or ankles.

4. You should alternate both leads and diagonals on trail rides. A horse who is permitted to canter on one lead continuously often becomes one-leaded and is unwilling to take the opposite lead. It is better for the development of your horse's muscles if you change diagonals occasionally.

5. The important points to remember when you make an emergency dismount are:

- Kick *both* feet out of the stirrups *before* you start to jump off your horse.
- Break your fall by keeping your right elbow across your horse's neck even after your feet touch the ground.
- Land facing the front of your horse and run a step or two forward.
- Keep hold of the reins.

Dangerous mistakes:

- Do not kick your feet free of the stirrups at the same time you are in the air. These are two distinct steps to the dismount: your feet first, your body second.
- Do not kick your horse as you jump off.
- Do not land facing the rear of your horse.
- Do not land hard. You can hurt your feet and legs if

you do not flex your knees and ankles as you land.
• Do not fall down. You should be able to keep your balance after you jump off.
• Do not let go of the reins. You might have a long walk home.

6. Circle at a canter.
    • Your horse should canter at a slow pace, completely under control.
    • You should be balanced, upright, and sitting to his canter.
    • You should be leaning the direction your horse leans on turns.

Common mistakes:
    • Your horse should not rush his canter, nor break out of the circle.
    • You should not bounce out of the saddle.
    • Your arms and legs should not move or flap.

7. Safety rules for trail riding.
    • Avoid riding bareback.
    • If you ride with a group, keep at least five feet behind the horse in front of you.
    • When you cross a street, all the horses in the group should line up on one side of the road facing the street. Then they should all cross the street at the same time.
    • Keep your horse's head up and keep him moving when you cross water.
    • Do not ride double.
    • Usually the best way to help a rider in trouble is to keep your horse out of his way and quiet. You may be able to block the path if the horse behind you bolts.

An experienced rider may be able to cut off a runaway horse to make him stop. Never be afraid to ask for help.

• A tree branch or bushes should be allowed to brush against your body as you pass. If you hold a branch in your hand until you have passed the tree, and then let go suddenly, it may snap in the face of the rider behind you.

• A horse leans into his curves and you should keep your balance with his.

Be wise when you are on a trail ride. It is not the place to try something new with your horse or to act funny. Be sure you get permission to ride on other people's property. Be polite so that others welcome riders. Always close gates behind you if you open them. If your horse spooks, let him investigate and face anything that frightens him. Be conscious of taking care of your horse and he will take care of you.

11
Yellow Ribbon Test

Riding section:

1. Pass the trail test.
*2. Canter a horse bareback. Stop from a canter.
3. Mount a horse bareback without assistance.
4. Demonstrate how to mount a horse that is difficult to mount, such as one that backs, turns, or moves while the rider is mounting.
5. While you are trotting around the ring, post without your stirrups.
*6. Demonstrate how to canter on both leads.

Horsemanship section:

1. How long should a horse stand after he has had grain before you should ride him?
2. Should your horse be given sugar. apples, carrots? How do you feed him tidbits?
3. How often should you exercise your horse?
4. Is it bad for a horse to be hot when he returns to the barn?
5. If your horse is sweating, should he be given a cold drink of water?

6. Would you turn your horse out to pasture while he was sweating?

7. If your horse has been eating hay, will it hurt him to be turned out to pasture?

HOW TO JUDGE YOUR PROFICIENCY ON THE YELLOW RIBBON TEST

Riding section:

1. Pass the trail test. You should also go on several trail rides.

2. You should be as balanced when you canter bareback as when you canter with a saddle.
   - You should be able to sit erect on your horse.
   - You should be able to make your horse canter at the place you ask.
   - Your horse should stop where you ask.

Common mistakes:
   - You should not become so tense you bounce while you canter bareback.
   - You should not slip around or need to hold the mane at a fast trot if your horse trots before you begin to canter.
   - You should not need to hold the mane to keep your balance.
   - You should not slip off because you failed to hold the mane in an emergency.
   - You should not need to lean forward to make your horse canter.
   - You should not lose your balance when your horse stops.

• You should not lose control of your horse.

Although the test specifies knowing how to canter bareback, you should be relaxed and in control no matter what your horse does. You may bounce if your horse trots, but you should not appear to be in danger of falling off. It is important to make your horse obey and to ride with ease at a canter.

3. In order to mount your horse bareback without assistance, find a hill and keep him lower on the hill than you are. A rock, a log, or a fence can be used for a mounting block.

4. When you mount a horse who turns, or backs, or walks forward while you are trying to mount:
• You should time your swing onto the saddle. First make him stand still by using your reins. The instant he is still, before he realizes you are not using two hands to make him obey, swing onto his back. You must be quick, confident and exact in your movements.
• You should make certain your horse stands still as soon as you mount.
• You may need to turn around with your horse and take an extra hop while one foot is in the stirrup. Keep a check on the reins even while your horse is turning. If he backs, back him in a corner and walk straight forward as soon as you mount.
• Be patient.

Common mistakes:
• The worst mistake is to be unable to mount.
• You should not become upset. If you keep trying, you will manage to mount no matter how much the horse wants to prevent you from succeeding.

• You should not put one foot in the stirrup until the horse is under control.

• You should not forget to keep one rein tighter than the other if your horse is turning while you are trying to mount.

5. When you post without your stirrups:

• Your thighs should rest slightly higher on the saddle than normal to give you support for posting.

• You should post on the correct diagonal.

• You should be relaxed.

• Your reins should be even and without tension.

Common mistakes:

• You should not be tense or stiff in the saddle.

• You should not forget to check your diagonals if you reverse.

6. When you canter on the correct lead:

• You should use leg pressure on the outside to ask for a canter. You use whichever rein your horse has been trained to accept as the signal for a canter. Some horses take the correct lead when you lift on the inside rein just at the moment you use leg pressure on the outside. Others take the correct lead when you lift on the outside rein.

• You should sit erect when you canter.

Common mistakes:

• You should not jerk on your horse's mouth when you ask for a lead.

• You should not forget to check to see if your horse took the correct lead.

- Your horse should not change leads while he is cantering. You should notice if he does, stop him, and take the correct lead again.
- You should not lean forward while you are cantering.

Horsemanship section:

1. A horse should stand a half hour to an hour after he has eaten before he is ridden. You should not ride a horse hard just after he has had his grain.

2. Sugar is not good for your horse. Carrots and apples may be fed as treats. It is best to feed him tidbits with his grain. However, if you do feed him with your fingers, hold the treat on the palm of your hand with your fingers flat so that he will not bite your fingers instead of the apple.

3. A horse should be able to move about each day. He should have regular exercise at least once a week. An hour's ride or turning him out to run for an hour or so every day is the best way to keep him healthy and content.

4. A horse should be cool before he is left to stand in his stall. You may walk your horse until he is cool or bathe and rub him down after a ride. If he is still hot after he is rubbed down, you should walk him until he is cool.

5. A horse should be cool before he drinks heavily.

6. You may turn your horse out to pasture on a warm summer day even if he is sweating. If it is cold and there is food in pasture so that he will be standing still to eat, cool him off first.

7. Of course, you may turn your horse out to pasture if he has been eating hay, unless it is spring and he is not used to grass.

12

Red Ribbon Test

Riding section:

*1. Demonstrate three speeds of the trot: slow, normal, and extended.

*2. Demonstrate how to keep your horse at a steady gait at a walk, a trot, and a canter.

3. Trot a figure eight, showing where to change diagonals.

4. Make the following program ride:
   a. trot half-way around the ring
   b. stop
   c. back six steps
   d. walk, then canter to a mid-point in the side of the ring
   e. trot to the corner and cut diagonally across the ring at a trot
   f. stop in the corner

*5. Reverse at a canter.

*6. Demonstrate good hands and seat while you are trotting and changing diagonals every five steps.

*7. Demonstrate good hands and seat when you canter, walk, reverse, and canter again.

8. Demonstrate how to back a horse a single step at a time.

Horsemanship section:

1. If you are doing a fast trot in a ring, where should your horse extend?
2. What should you remember when stopping from a slow trot?
3. What is the purpose of a program ride?
4. If you are riding in a horse show:
   a. Why should you keep your distance from other horses?
   b. Should you watch the judge?
   c. Should you continue cantering if another rider is having trouble with his horse?
   d. When the ringmaster gives a command, do you obey when the other horses obey or when you hear the command?
   e. What will the judge be looking at when you walk? when you trot? when you canter?
   f. Why does the judge have you trot and canter in each direction?
   g. Where do you line up after a class?
   h. What should you do if your horse wins and your number is called?
5. If you fall off a horse in a horse show, what should you do? If you fall off at other times, what should you do?

HOW TO JUDGE YOUR PROFICIENCY ON THE RED RIBBON TEST

Riding section:

1. For three speeds of a trot:

At a *slow* trot:
 • You should sit in the saddle without posting.

• Your horse should keep in a slow trot at a steady pace.
• You should resume a normal trot before you stop trotting.

Common mistakes:

• You should not let your horse slow to a walk or speed up to a normal trot.
• You should not need to keep tension on the reins while you are doing a slow trot, although you may need to check your horse occasilonally, keeping a light contact.
• Your hands should not waver up and down because you are bouncing, nor should you be tightening and loosening the reins at each step.
• You should not be bouncing in the saddle while you are trotting. If you are relaxed, your seat will be steady.
• The pace should not be a shuffle, but light, dancing steps, although he is trotting at a slower than normal trot.

At a *normal* trot:

• You should maintain a steady pace that is natural to your horse.

Common mistakes:

• It is counted as a mistake if you do not know when your horse has taken a normal trot.
• You should not allow your horse to change his speed, cut corners, or get close to other horses.
• You should not forget to post on the correct diagonal.
• Your position should not be sloppy.

At a *fast* trot:
- Your horse should extend his legs as he trots. This gait is often called an extended trot.
- You should slow your horse to a normal trot on curves.
- Leg pressure should be used to keep him in an extended trot.
- You should be able to see his front legs shooting straight out in front of him. The horse's strides are longer so that you feel suspended in the air more than you are touching the ground.

Common mistakes:
- You should not need to keep tension on the reins all the time you are trotting in order to prevent your horse from cantering, although you must have the feel of his mouth.
- Your horse should not canter.
- It is counted as a mistake if you cannot tell when your horse is extending.
- You should not permit your horse to cut corners, come close to other horses, or make a circle of his own on the inside of the ring rather than following the fence.
- You should not lose control.
- You should not become tense, stiff, or excited while you are taking a fast trot.

You will understand how your horse moves and how to control his movements better when you are able to take three speeds of the trot. The most common mistakes riders make are forgetting to sit to the slow trot, and trotting fast around corners in an extended trot.

2. A rider in a show ring or a class of instruction should be "riding" his horse all the time. The horse should take his pace because the rider directs him.

At a *walk*:
- Your horse should be alert. He should be ready to change gaits immediately.
- He should be walking at a normal pace. You should feel his hind legs giving propulsion.

Common mistakes:
- Your horse should not be lagging, walking along with his eyes half closed.
- Leg pressure or a shove with your heel should not startle him into wakefulness.

At a *trot*:
- Your horse should move willingly and steadily.
- The rhythm of your posting should be unvaried.
- Your horse should be responsive to any change of direction.

Common mistakes:
- Your horse should not slow down as if he were about to stop, nor should he fight your control and try to canter.
- He should not change his pace from a slow to an extended trot and back to a slow trot again.
- He should not balk although you keep him trotting for extended periods of ten or fifteen minutes.
- He should not wander where he likes as he trots, but should trot smartly beside the fence, wide of other horses, and into the corners. If you are trotting with

a group of horses, he should not trot with the other horses but independently at a distance from them.

At a *canter*:
- Your horse should take his canter when you ask and sustain it until you ask him to stop.
- He should be on the correct lead.
- He should canter quietly, steadily, with a rocking rhythm.
- You should have control at all times.
- Your horse should canter where you want.
- You should have good hands and seat.
- Your horse should be collected, with his neck slightly bent and his hind legs coming underneath him for propulsion.

Common mistakes:
- You should not have trouble keeping your horse in a canter.
- Your horse should not rush around the ring.
- He should not be difficult to stop.
- He should not have his head really high or strung out ahead of him.

Precision is the word that best describes a steady rider. You need to be alert all the time you are riding to bring out the best qualities in your horse. Your horse should be responsive, willing, and eager to please you, because he knows you will not tolerate slackness on his part. Not only should he obey your signals to trot, canter and stop, but he should feel your control so that he goes exactly where you want him to go at the speed you want without obvious signals or effort on your part.

3. When you trot a figure eight:
  • You should indicate where you will trot the figure and then trot it where you have outlined.
  • Your circles will be round.
  • You will begin in the center of the figure eight, loop, and stop in the center after you have completed the figure.
  • Your horse should trot at a steady pace.
  • You should change diagonals before each loop of the eight.

Common mistakes:
  • You should not trot a lop-sided figure eight.
  • You should not forget to change diagonals.
  • Your horse should not stop while you are trotting the figure eight.
  • You should not have trouble controlling your horse. He should not trot too fast, leave the area where you want to trot, or fight your directions.

A figure eight gives you practice working your horse independently, in curves, and in precise figures. It makes him more supple. It shows you how to use your weight, your hands, and you legs with the least effort to get the most response from your horse. In a show the judge usually checks diagonals when you trot a figure eight. He assumes you have control.

4. A program ride tests your ability to follow directions exactly and to have obedience from your horse when you ask him to change gaits or directions. If you are testing yourself, make up various program rides and then execute them.

This program ride tests your skill to make your horse take three gaits and to back. You should judge your proficiency by how well you keep him under control even in the center of the ring.

During the program ride:
• You should have good seat and hands throughout the ride.
• The signals you give your horse should be quiet, almost unnoticeable.
• Your horse should change gaits as soon as you ask and stop exactly where you ask.
• He should stay close to the fence when he is working beside it. When he is crossing the ring, he should trot straight.
• He should have the correct lead.
• You should post on the correct diagonal.
• He should back and take his leads willingly, without hesitation.

Common mistakes:
• You should not fail to make your horse trot, stop or canter exactly at the designated points.
• You should not lose control.
• You should not bump into another horse, touch a fence, or meander from one point to the next.

When you back your horse during the program ride:
• Your horse should back easily and should back straight.
• Your weight should be back, your head up, your eyes forward.
• You should use equal leg pressure.

* You should pull evenly on both reins.

Common mistakes:
   * You should not jerk on your horse's mouth.
   * Your reins should not be uneven.
   * You should not look down at your hands or at your horse.
   * Your horse should not back too many or too few steps.
   * You should not have both legs pressing in if your horse begins to back crooked. One leg should press harder to straighten out his hindquarters.

5. When you reverse at a canter:
   * You should take the correct lead when you begin to canter.
   * As you reverse, you should trot two or three steps before taking the other lead.

Common mistakes:
   * Your horse should not make a flying change (changing leads while he is cantering).
   * Your horse should not canter into the center of the ring.
   * He should not rush his canter.
   * You should not let him change leads himself. If he takes the wrong lead, you should stop and take the canter again.
   * You should not lean forward to get your leads or to check if you are in the correct lead.

The main purpose of this section of the test is to prove you are able to take the correct lead with your horse in either direction. You also need to know how to reverse correctly at a canter.

6. When you change diagonals every five steps:
   • You need excellent balance. You cannot be dependent on your hands for balance. You must be secure in your seat.
   • You may change diagonals by sitting or standing a beat, but you should know how to do it either way.
   • You will need a sense of timing. You should feel your horse's steps and know without looking down that you are posting on the correct diagonal.
   • You should know which diagonal you are on all the time.

Common mistakes:
   • You should not miss your timing while you are posting, nor miss making a change of diagonals.
   • You should not jerk on the reins nor move your hands when you post or change diagonals.
   • You should not lose control of your horse.
   • You should not let your horse change his pace.

Although this part of the test appears to examine what you know about diagonals, it is really a test of your balance. It is important that you ride smoothly, do not interfere with your horse's mouth, and make your change of diagonals appear effortless.

7. When you demonstrate good seat and hands at a canter in either direction:
   • You should use your legs, hands and weight correctly to get your lead.

- You should take the canter from the walk with no visible effort on your part.
- You should be sitting erect while you take the canter and while you are cantering.
- You should be able to feel if you are on the correct lead, rather than leaning forward to look.
- Your riding should appear effortless. This means you feel relaxed, are able to sit the canter easily, and have such good control of your horse that you do not have to work to make him obey.

Common mistakes:
- You should not be mistaken in your leads.
- You should not need to kick your horse. You should be able to make him canter without using your heels by the time you are a Red Ribbon Rider.

This section of the test lets you show your ability to sit erect and feel how your horse moves at a canter without dropping your eyes to make sure he is on the correct lead.

8. Backing one step at a time, or controlled backing, involves:
- Pressure on the reins until your horse starts to yield, then releasing immediately so that he only takes one step.
- Quiet hands that give steady pressure on the reins.
- Leg pressure only while you have tension on the reins.

Common mistakes:
- Your horse should not back with both front legs as

if this were a single step. This means he has taken two steps.

• You should not look down.

Horsemanship section:

1. A horse taking an extended trot should slow to a normal trot on curves. He is better balanced at a normal trot, therefore safer, when he takes a sharp turn.

2. Usually you should take a normal trot before you stop from a slow trot. You do not want your horse to associate a slow trot with stopping. However, in a show you must walk immediately after the slow trot if the judge asks for a walk.

3. A program ride indicates how well a rider controls his horse. It also shows his ability to change gaits and directions when he wants.

4. In a horse show:

a. You keep away from other horses not only to avoid accidents but to allow the judge to see you work your horse. A judge notices the riders who are able to keep their horses out of the bunch.

b. You should not watch the judge. You should always look where you are going.

c. In a professional horse show, if a rider is having trouble with her horse you should give her as much room as possible while you continue in the gait called for. In a private horse show, such as one at a camp, you should stop until the rider has his horse under control.

d. Always obey the instructions of the ringmaster as soon as they are given.

e. A judge watches your seat and hands, how you control your horse, and whether you know leads and diagonals.

f. A judge has you trot in both directions to see if you know diagonals. He has you canter in both directions to see if you are able to take both leads.

g. You should line up facing the judge or facing the direction he asks.

h. You should walk forward a few steps to let the judge pin your horse if your number is called.

5. If you fall off your horse, mount again and continue to ride. Most judges give you a few minutes to recover your equilibrium before they watch how you ride again.

All riders fall off sometime. It is important to mount and ride again. If you are afraid of the horse or he is hurt, ride another horse for a few minutes until you conquer your fear. Of course, if you are seriously hurt, you should not try to ride immediately.

13

Blue Ribbon Test

Riding section:

*1. Canter a figure eight.
2. Change leads in a straight line.
*3. Demonstrate a relaxed, assured seat and good hands while you walk, trot, canter.
4. Take a hand gallop.
5. Lead a trail ride.
6. Take part in a horseshow.
7. Take part in a group game on horseback.
*8. Trot a figure eight with a partner.
*9. Canter and reverse at a canter with a partner.

Horsemanship section:

1. Should a horse be groomed before you ride him every time?
2. What are the most important parts of a horse to clean?
3. How much hay should you give your horse? How much water?
4. How can you tell how much grain to give your horse?
5. What else is essential for his diet?

6. How often should your horse be fed?

7. Does a pony need grain?

8. Can a horse be stabled in a cold barn during the winter?

9. When the grass first comes up in the spring, is it good for your horse to be turned out all day?

10. How often should your horse be shod? Does he have to be shod?

11. Is it safe to ride your horse in the snow?

Instructor's section:

(To be used with groups of riders.)

1. Help teach a beginner for three days.

2. Assist with a trail ride.

3. Work in the stable area for six days.

4. Be recommended for safety consciousness, cooperation, and setting a good example for other riders.

It is difficult to give a Blue Ribbon Test. A rider needs to have high quality in his performance, rather than an acquisition of new skills. It is easy to judge when a rider has learned how to post, because you can see him post, but it is difficult to say when a rider reverses at a canter with the skill of a Red Ribbon Rider and when he does it so effortlessly he is a Blue Ribbon Rider.

One criterion can be used. No rider is ready to pass his Blue Ribbon Test within two weeks of taking his Red Ribbon Test. Hours of careful work and intensive instruction should precede this final test.

Another gauge is attitude. The rider who thinks he knows everything there is to learn about riding is unlikely to be as skilled as he feels he is.

A Blue Ribbon Rider will know how to make any horse responsive. He has confidence about riding cross country. He knows how to cope with whatever a horse may do. He is always kind to horses. His seat is relaxed, his hands gentle. A Blue Ribbon Rider should know something about jumping, although jumping is included in a separate section of these tests.

HOW TO JUDGE YOUR PROFICIENCY ON THE BLUE RIBBON TEST

Riding section:

1. When you canter a figure eight:
   - You should start going in a circle to the right.
   - Your horse should take a controlled canter.
   - You should be "riding" him all the time—he should obey you perfectly when you ask for the canter, when you change leads, when you stop, and while you are cantering.
   - He should start his canter within a step or two of the center of the eight. When he finishes the first loop of the eight, he should only need two or three trotting steps before he takes the other lead. He should stop exactly in the center of the eight when he finishes the figure.
   - Your circles should be round and the same size. Your horse should follow your plan of where you intend to canter the eight.
   - Your riding should appear effortless. Your seat should be secure, relaxed.

Common mistakes:

• You should not have to struggle to get your horse into a canter, nor to take the correct lead for either loop of the figure eight. If you do have a difficult horse to manage, you should have sufficient control to get the leads, to keep him within the circles of the eight (although you may make larger loops than when you ride a better trained horse), and he should stop exactly in the center when you finish the eight.

• Your horse should not get out of control. You have lost control if your horse elongates either circle of the eight, needs to be tugged to stay in the circle, canters too fast, or does not stop when you finish the eight.

• Your horse should not refuse to take either lead, nor should he take an incorrect lead.

• When you begin your figure eight, do not go in the wrong direction because your horse takes the left lead.

• You should not lean forward to get your leads.

• You should not need to hold your horse under tight control to keep him collected while he is cantering.

• Your horse should not break into a trot while he is on one of the loops of the eight.

• You should not let him change leads while he is cantering.

• He should not be disunited while he is cantering.

• Your aids should be very subtle so that someone watching cannot see them.

A figure eight at a canter should appear easy for your horse, easy for you. You should use a small enough area for it to be obvious that you are directing your horse into an eight and not just cantering circles in a large field. The eight should be exact. Sloppiness in the way you canter the eight or in your position should mean failure on this test.

2. In order to change leads in a straight line you should take the canter on one lead, trot two or three steps in the center of the line, and take the other lead without turning your horse.
   • Your horse should canter straight across the center of the ring.
   • You should have control of him.

Common mistakes:
   • You should not take whichever lead he chooses first, but have him take the lead you direct him to take.
   • You should not need to kick your horse.
   • You should not lack precision when you ask for the canter, or when you change leads.

3. A Blue Ribbon Rider has a relaxed seat. His hands are resilient, quiet, assured. His horse responds to those hands, yet is never hampered by them. His seat is balanced at all gaits, especially when changing gaits.

Bad habits:
   • You should not watch your horse while you are riding; you should feel him.
   • You should not have hard hands. You can tell hard hands by jerking movements, sudden tugs on the bit, inflexible wrists, fingers tightened into fists, reins that go slack and then tight as the horse moves, elbows that are tight against a rider's sides or that do not bend and straighten naturally when the rider posts.
   • You should not fail to watch small details such as

twisted stirrup leathers, incorrectly fastened tack, uneven reins, the bight on the wrong side of the neck,
feet that slip to the outside of the stirrups.
• You should not let yourself become overconfident.
Cockiness is a danger, and an obstacle to learning.

4. In a hand gallop:
   • You should stand in your galloping position, but still
   remain close to the saddle.
   • You should have a light contact on your horse's
   mouth.
   • You should look forward.

Common mistakes:
   • You should not lose your balance, let your weight
   slip back, or tug on the reins for balance or security.
   • Your hands should not rest or your horse's neck.
   • You should not let your horse gallop over rough
   ground.
   • You should not take half the ring to stop your horse.

Since a hand gallop is simply an extended canter, you
should have the same control and assurance you have at a
normal canter.

5. When you are leading a trail ride:
   • You should take responsibility for the safety and
   pleasure of those with you.
   • You should help instruct the riders.
   • Before you start the ride, you should be sure every-
   one understands the rules for safety on trail.

A Blue Ribbon Rider will be more interested in the
progress of the riders on his trail ride than in himself. He

should be able to make the trail fun without feeling it is necessary to canter continuously. The horses should be cool when he returns.

6. When you enter a horse show:
   • You should show concern for the appearance of your horse so that he is properly groomed. Your tack should be clean and in good condition.
   • During the show, you should be courteous. You should be a good sport whether you win or lose.

A horse show often teaches you your weaknesses and gives you a standard by which to measure your progress. Remember that the horse's performance will determine how well you place just as much as your riding skill. You may need to train your horse for a horse show before you are in the ribbons.

7. A group game should not be played just for fun. Your horse should learn to respond quickly to signals. You should remember to be considerate of your horse. Fair play and sportsmanship are such an important part of riding; they should be of primary importance when you are playing a game.

8. When you trot a figure eight:
   • Keep boot to boot with your partner all the time you are trotting.
   • Trot slowly enough when you are on the inside of one loop to make it easy for your partner to trot on the outside. Urge your horse into a fast enough trot when you are on the outside of the other loop to allow your partner to trot easily. He should not be forced to walk to stay beside you.

• You should have light control on your horse's mouth while you are trotting.
• Be sure you change diagonals for each loop of the eight.
• Be sure you stop together.

Common mistakes:
• You should not blame your partner for mistakes. If you match your riding to his, no one will detect the mistakes.
• Do not continue to trot if your partner falls behind. Wait for him. Keep together.
• You should not lose control of your horse.
• You should not trot outside of the boundary of the figure eight.
• You should not need to kick your horse.
• You should not jerk on your horse's mouth.

You often discover your weaknesses in control when you ride with a partner. You need to have perfect control to trot a figure eight as a pair. It should look easy.

9. When you canter with a partner:
• Watch each other's horses. Begin your canter together. Stop together.
• Ride boot to boot.
• Be sure you decide which direction you will reverse and stay together when you do it. Take your trot at the same time in the middle of your reverse.
• Be sure you have the correct lead.
• Your position should be correct.
• Your hands should be light.

Common mistakes:
- You should not lose control.
- You should not canter independently of your partner, nor ride ahead of or behind him.
- You should not become provoked with your partner's mistakes.
- You should not kick your horse.
- You should not lean forward when you are cantering.

This is a difficult exercise, especially since one rider is usually better than the other. You should practice and help your partner until you are able to keep with him throughout the entire figure.

Horsemanship section:

1. A horse feels good when he is clean, just as people do. Grooming also conditions his muscles. The best way to keep him clean is to groom him every day. He does not need grooming every time you ride, if you ride several times a day, but he should be "touched up" with a brush and curry where the saddle and girth go.
2. The most important parts of a horse to keep clean are the places where he is most likely to get sore: under the saddle and girth, especially right behind his forelegs where the skin bunches up against the girth, behind his pasterns, and his feet.
3. A horse eats about a bale of hay a day. He should have all the water he wants to drink.
4. A horse needs enough grain to keep his weight and his pep. The amount varies with each horse. If your horse becomes nasty and uncontrollable, you may be giving him too much grain. If he begins to look boney, you may not

be giving him enough grain, or he may have worms.

5. A horse must have salt in his diet.

6. Horses are usually grained twice a day.

7. Most ponies do not need grain.

8. A horse may be kept in an unheated barn. If he is clipped, he should have a blanket for cold weather.

9. A horse should not have all the grass he wants to eat the first day he is turned out to pasture. Begin with twenty minutes grazing a day and increase the length of time gradually each day. Otherwise the sudden richness in his diet could cause colic.

10. Horses need to be reshod or reset every six to eight weeks. If a horse is only ridden on soft earth, he does not need shoes, but he will need to have his feet trimmed occasionally.

11. Most horses can be ridden without shoes in the snow, but there are special shoes also that make winter riding safe. Your horse knows if it is too slippery or if the crust will not hold him, and hesitates to venture out. Wait for a thaw.

Instructor's section:

1. Experienced riders should feel an interest in helping less experienced riders learn. As an instructor, you need as much help as you can get to manage groups of riders. Few children are natural teachers. They tend to be bossy or to act superior. Supervise them closely if they are used as assistant teachers. Outline the tasks you want taught such as leading horses for small children, holding horses in the ring, helping a class to mount, teaching beside a more experienced teacher, working in the stable.

2. An advanced rider should know how to lead a trail ride,

what to do to make the ride safe, where a group is permitted to ride. An instructor should always supervise the ride; she may bring up the rear or teach individuals in line.

3. An advanced rider needs to have a period of day by day exposure to the operations in a stable. He needs to know the needs of the horses, the system used to feed them, bed them, exercise them. This period of working with horses will help him see the relationship between the care a horse is given and the horse's performance in the ring.

4. One of the most important lessons you can teach a rider is to be conscious of what makes him safe when he is working with or riding horses. This safety sense should include everyone around him.

A rider should cooperate during lessons and when he is in the stable area, not just to make teaching easier for you, but to enable him to get along with his companions, future teachers, and judges in the show ring.

Your advanced riders, so admired by all those who aspire to ride as well as they do, must set a good example when they are riding and when they are working with horses. Anything an advanced rider does is likely to be imitated. He may be responsible for other riders' improvements, or he can, through carelessness, cause an accident. He should understand the responsibility that is his.

A note to instructors about jumping: If you wish to include jumping with your advanced riding tests, do not include jumping with the White Ribbon Test for advanced riders. This test is designed primarily to judge a rider's ability to canter.

Part IV

TESTS FOR JUMPING

14
White Ribbon Test

1. Show how you make a correct approach to a jump.
2. Demonstrate the correct position for jumping while you trot over a bar on the ground.
3. Show what to do with your horse after the jump.
4. Trot over a 4″ jump. Make a correct approach, show proper form over the jump, and control after the jump.
°5. Canter over a 4″-8″ jump correctly.
6. Explain the safety rules to remember when jumping including:
   a. Should you use a hard hat?
   b. What is the purpose of a forward position for jumping?
   c. How does a rider keep a secure seat when a horse balks, jumps too soon, or hits the bar?
   d. What should the rider be prepared to do if his horse falls?
   e. Before he jumps, what precautionary measures should a rider take?

HOW TO JUDGE YOUR PROFICIENCY ON THE WHITE RIBBON TEST

1. In order to make a correct approach to a jump:
   • You should look at the jump before you turn toward it.
   • Your horse should move at a steady gait, whether you take the jump at a trot during practice or at a canter.
   • He should be alert and moving well.
   • He should come straight into the jump.
   • He should respond to your leg pressure to make an effort at the jump when you ask.

Common mistakes:
   • Your horse should not rush his jumps, nor should he lag as he comes toward them.
   • You should feel if he starts to run out and correct him before he is able to pass outside the jump.
   • If he intends to balk, you should feel him slowing down or notice the reluctance in his steps, and use leg pressure (your heels if necessary) to make him jump.
   • If you do not have control, you should not take your horse over the jump. Circle and approach again.

Your horse must be alert and moving easily as he comes into a jump. Exact control is the most important step toward good jumping. It is as wrong to let him rush a jump as to let him break into a trot from a canter and make a half-hearted attempt to jump. The approach to the jump *is* the jump most of the time. You can tell if your horse is responding to you, eager, and ready for the jump.

2. The correct position for jumping puts you forward in your saddle.
- Your heels should be down, with give in your ankles.
- Your knees should be slightly bent, your legs underneath you in the same position they are in when you are sitting in the saddle.
- Your back is straight as you stand.
- Your shoulders should be further forward than your buttocks.
- For beginning jumping, your hands should be on the mane, with one rein in each hand.
- Your elbows should be bent so that your arms feel relaxed.
- There should be resilience in your body, your arms, your legs, your ankles.
- Your head should be up so that you are looking forward.

Common mistakes:
- You should never become tense or stiff while jumping.
- Your heels should not go up as you trot over the bar.
- You should not let your legs swing forward so that you sit down in the saddle.
- You should not let your heels go up or your legs swing backward, so that you fall on the horse's neck.
- You should not look down at the jump.
- You should not take your hands off the mane.
- You should not lose your balance before, during, or after the practice jump.

Form on practice jumps, with the bar on the ground, should be perfect before you raise the bar. It is important that you keep a firm hold on the mane and that your heels stay down on every practice jump. As long as you keep your heels down, you are unlikely to lose your balance and hit your horse. With your hands on the mane, you will not jerk on the reins if you do lose your balance.

3. After your horse finishes a single jump:
   • He should continue at the same gait and pace he used before the jump.
   • He should go straight away from the jump.
   • When you are well beyond the jump, you should stop your horse.
   • Your horse should be under control.
   • You should remain in your galloping position for several steps beyond the jump.

Common mistakes:
   • You should not look back at the jump to see if your horse knocked down the bar.
   • You should not let your horse bolt or stop as soon as he finishes jumping.
   • Your horse should not turn aside as he comes down from the jump.

It is important to make your horse do whatever you ask after a jump because you will need his obedience on jump courses. If he gets in the habit of turning immediately after a jump, he may begin to jump crooked. If he stops after a jump, you will have difficulty taking him over a jump course. You will need to control his gait between jumps on a course, so you need to begin with your practice jumps controlling his speed after he crosses the bar.

4. When you trot over a 4″ jump, your horse will pick up his feet slightly to give you the feel of the jump.
• You must have control of your horse as you come into the jump.
• You should have correct form over the jump.
• After the jump, you should keep your horse trotting straight at a steady pace.
• You should take your galloping position well ahead of the jump, hold it over the jump and for several steps after the jump.

Common mistakes:
• You should not forget the importance of *each* phase of the jump: the smooth approach, form over the jump, control after the jump.
• Your horse should not rush the jump; nor should he bolt through it rather than jumping.
• He should not walk as soon as he goes over the jump.
• It is a major error to let your heels go up as you go over the jump.
• It is equally wrong to let go of the mane or to fall back on your horse.

A preliminary jump of 4″ tests your ability to keep your balance and to think of many things at once. If you make a major mistake, such as losing control, or jerking on your horse, or falling back on him, you should practice a great deal before you try the same size jump at a canter.

5. When you canter over a 4″ jump, if your horse does

not actually jump, raise the bar a couple of inches until he does jump it. You should not need to raise it more than 8″ as a rule to make him jump.

- Your horse should make a good approach.
- He should be under control.
- He should canter at a steady pace, neither rushing and fighting your control, nor lagging so there is a chance of his trotting or balking.
- He should pick up for the jump when you ask.
- You should stay in a galloping position for several steps before, as well as over and after the jump. When you are secure in this position, you will be able to make one jump after another without losing your balance and without being jarred as your horse lands.

Common mistakes:

- You should not let your seat hit the saddle as your horse lands.
- Your horse should not take the wrong lead.
- Your form should not become lax so that you forget where you are looking, your heels, your hands on the mane, etc.

You should have control of your horse when you begin jumping the bar at a canter. The first symptom of your lack of control is if you allow your horse to cut corners or to come into the jump at an angle. If he rushes the jump or you need to ride the reins all the way into the jump, you do not have control. The way to judge whether you have mastered the fundamentals of beginning jumping is to check that you keep both your balance and control. The tendency to let your horse do the work without making an effort yourself, failure to use leg pressure or to kick if necessary to motivate him so that he actually jumps the bar, are major faults. Until you have control, balance and the correct motivation of your horse, you should not pass this test.

6. A few of the safety rules for jumping:

a. Always wear a hard hat.

b. If a rider is in his galloping position, his center of balance is with the horse's. This helps the horse keep his balance as he jumps. The rider will not fall on his horse's back during the landing, nor will he slip forward to strike the pommel of the saddle.

c. A rider who is secure in his seat will have his heels down, his thighs close to the saddle, so that he cannot be jarred off balance no matter what the horse does.

d. A rider should immediately get both feet out of the stirrups and be prepared to make an emergency dismount if his horse falls. He should roll away *fast* from the horse.

e. Always check the girth before jumping. Stirrups should be one hole shorter for jumping than for riding on the flat.

15
Yellow Ribbon Test

*1. Canter your horse over a one foot jump (with your hands on the mane).

2. How do you seesaw on the reins as you come into a jump? When do you use this technique?

*3. How do you keep an eager horse calm as you approach the jump?

*4. What methods do you use to make a stubborn horse jump?

*5. Demonstrate how to jump with your horse: when to take off and when to come into the saddle.

6. Canter over a low in and out jump.

7. What do you do if your horse knocks down the bar?

HOW TO JUDGE YOUR PROFICIENCY ON THE YELLOW RIBBON TEST

1. You should be able to take a one foot jump easily with your hands on the mane.

• You should have control coming into the jump as well as after the jump.

- Your reins should be long enough as you go over the jump to give your horse his head.
- You should maintain correct form over the jump.

Common mistakes:
- Your horse should approach the jump at a steady pace. If he slows down, loses his canter, or balks, *you* have not brought him into the jump correctly.
- If he runs out on the jump, you did not have control.
- You should not jerk on his mouth because you lost your grip on the mane or held the reins too tight.
- You should not lose your balance so that you fall forward or backward.
- After the jump, you should not let yourself into the saddle so soon that you hit your horse.
- Your horse should not trot, or canter, too fast after the jump.

When you take this test, your horse should be jumping the bar. Your approach should be smooth, your control good. You should make your horse jump with leg pressure or a kick if he needs urging. The four faults which mean failure are: losing your hold on the mane, letting your heels go up, hitting your horse, losing control of your horse. Until you can make this elementary jump with your hands on the mane, you should not attempt other jumps.

2. Seesawing on the reins means putting tension on one rein as you release with the other.
- Your pulling and releasing should be smooth and definite so that the horse responds to each pull.
- As you approach a jump, you feel in your hands

whether your horse is moving willingly straight into the jump. If he is thinking about ducking out to one side or the other, you need to seesaw on the reins.
• It is a technique that helps keep a horse under control so that he comes straight into the jump.

Common mistakes:
• You should not jerk on the reins instead of pulling and releasing first one rein then the other.
• It is wrong to pull with both reins when you are trying to seesaw.
• You should not pull harder on one rein so that you make the horse run out to that side.
• You should not seesaw with the reins if your horse always runs to the same side. Instead of seesawing, you should be ready to check his move in one direction only by having that rein slightly shorter.
• You must not forget to give your horse his head when he goes over the jump because you are thinking so hard about controlling him before the jump.

Seesawing on the reins is one method of control. The worst mistake you can make is to continue to seesaw when your horse begins his jump.

3. There are various ways to calm an eager horse.
• You can work on control when you are not jumping.
• You can make practice jumps with the bar on the ground so that he comes between the standards quietly over and over again.
• As you approach the jump, you can use your weight (keeping it back) and your voice to quiet him. Your

hands must be firm but not hard as you strive for control.

• You can circle him before the jump if he is not coming into it quietly.

• You can bring him slowly into the jump until he is only a few canter steps from the standards before you release him to canter.

• After every jump you can bring him under control immediately.

Common mistakes:

• You should not allow your horse to rush his jumps again and again.

• If you cannot control your horse, you should not jump him.

• You should not lean forward during the approach.

• Your horse should not bolt after the jump.

• You are at fault if you lose your position or hurt your horse when he jumps. No matter how he takes his jump, you should go with him on the jump itself.

• You should not become impatient with your horse because he is slow to correct his over-eager attitude. Be glad he wants to jump.

It is important to have control before you learn to jump. It takes both you and your horse as a team working together to make jumping successful, so your horse must respond to you. Do not be eager to jump high, only to jump well.

4. Before trying to make a stubborn horse jump, be sure he has the ability to jump and is not stubborn because of

ignorance or because there is something wrong with him.

- Your approach to the jump will determine whether you are able to make a stubborn horse jump. Be sure he is awake and moving well before you approach the jump.
- You may need to push him with your legs, your heels, your crop, during the approach.
- He may only need a sharp reminder at the jump so that he makes the needed effort to pick up his feet.
- If he refuses the jump, you should use your crop to punish him, then immediately try the jump again.
- You may need to lower the bar.

Common mistakes:

- You must be sure that you are jumping correctly. If you are jerking on your horse's mouth or falling back hard on the saddle every time you jump, your horse will become an unwilling jumper.
- You may not have taken the needed time to teach your horse what a jump is before you asked him to jump too high.
- You may be using such a light bar on the jump he does not hit his legs hard enough to make him willing to try to jump.
- You may be leaning back during your approach so that you discourage his efforts.
- If you do not have control when you approach the jump, many horses know you cannot make them jump and will not try.
- If you approach the jump at an angle, your horse may not even realize you intend to go over an obstacle.
- If you always allow your horse to run out on a jump, or through it, he will not make an effort to jump.

• You should not pull on the reins at the same time you urge your horse to jump.

• Your hands should not be hard, nor your reins tight, as you urge your horse to jump.

The purpose of this part of the test is to show your ability to jump on a horse that is not an "automatic jumper." You cannot rely on your horse to make all his jumps perfectly without any direction from you. Jumping on a difficult horse early in your jumping experience teaches you what to demand of a horse and how to work with him.

5. Jumping "with your horse" means rising from the saddle when his forelegs leave the ground and coming into the saddle just after his hind legs touch earth on the far side of the jump.

• You should "feel" your horse take off, and should come out of the saddle as he lifts off with his forelegs.

• You should be resilient in the air, flexing as he lands to cushion the shock, and then sitting down before he has taken a stride.

• You should feel his forward motion as he jumps and go with it.

• Your hands should go forward to catch the mane as you rise from the saddle. The reins should be long enough to give your horse freedom of movement with his head and neck as he stretches over the jump.

• You should be relaxed as you jump.

Common mistakes:

• You will feel left behind if your horse takes off from

the ground and you do not rise from the saddle as he rises.

• If you come into the saddle too soon after the jump, you will hit your horse. If you come down too late, you will feel him take his first stride while you are still out of the saddle.

• You should not straighten your knees so much you are high off the saddle, off-balance and stiff.

• You should not lose your hold on the mane because you are thinking so hard about going with your horse.

• You should not interfere with your horse's head by having your reins too tight.

• You should not shift your weight in the air over the jump.

This section of the Yellow Ribbon tests your improvement in form. It separates you from White Ribbon Riders. You should gain a feeling of movement with your horse in order to time your rising from the saddle and sitting down again with the horse. Even if he takes off at the wrong time, you should go with him. At the same time, it is important to remember your control and not to interfere with his jump.

6. An in and out jump will have the standards close enough so that the horse takes one or two canter steps between the jumps. Both jumps should be less than a foot high for this test.

• You should have control over both jumps.

• You should remain in your galloping position between the jumps.

• You should think ahead to the second jump while you are still going over the first one.

Common mistakes:
- You should not relax after you go over the first jump, so that you are not ready for the second jump.
- You should not forget to go with your horse on the second jump as well as on the first.
- You should have enough impetus to take your horse over both jumps so that he does not stop after the first jump.
- Your horse should not run out between the jumps because you lost control.

An in and out is an introduction to multiple jumps. It is an extension of a single jump in the sense that it does not mean a change in your position, or a change in direction before the second jump. Control is your primary concern before you attempt a jump course.

7. If your horse knocks down the bar
- You should take the jump again immediately.
- Be sure your horse is moving willingly and well as he approaches the jump.
- You should be sure he times his jump correctly.
- You should use leg pressure or your heels at the jump to make him pick up for it.

Common mistakes:
- You should not repeat the mistakes you made the first time he refused. Your reins should not be tight; you should not let your horse lag as he approaches the jump; you should be sure he is coming straight into the jump.
- If your horse knocked the bar down because he

rushed through the jump, you should not let him run into it out of control a second time.

• You should not expect your horse to improve his performance without an effort on your part. You must be willing to push him, kick him, control him.

It is most important to take the jump again. Usually your problem is lack of control in some form.

16

Red Ribbon Test

1. Canter around the ring in your galloping position without touching the neck of your horse.

2. If a horse refuses to jump, how do you punish him?

3. What do you do if your horse runs out on the second jump of an in and out?

*4. Jump a series of in and outs with a barrier on either side.

*5. Jump 2½' with

    a. a bridge of the reins.

    b. your hands on the neck of your horse.

6. Make a 2' jump with a partner and his horse.

*7. Take your horse over a jump course in the woods where the highest jump is 2½' and there are at least four jumps. One of the jumps should be solid, such as a wall or a log.

8. Point out a horse that jumps too soon, too late, correctly.

HOW TO JUDGE YOUR PROFICIENCY
ON THE RED RIBBON TEST

1. You must be able to canter in your galloping position, balanced and at ease, before you try to take the Red Ribbon Test.

• Your touch on the reins should be so light that it does not interfere with the horse's forward motion while you still have the feel of the bit and therefore control of your horse. Your hands should follow his head movements.

• Your hands should be forward beside his neck, without touching it.

• Your elbows should be bent, your arms relaxed.

• You should be standing in the saddle, your knees slightly bent.

• You should be "light in the thighs" so that your body gives with the motion of the canter.

• Your weight should be in your heels, not in your knees.

Common mistakes:

• You should not be tense. Tenseness shows in an overall stiffness, in tight reins, hard hands, or in a jarring through your body at each canter step.

• You should not pinch the saddle between your knees.

• You should not use your reins to catch your balance.

• You should not need to grab the neck or the mane to keep your balance.

• You should be so secure in this position that your legs do not swing back, your knees do not flip out, your heels do not go up, your stirrups do not flop, or your legs do not go forward so you sit down.

This is an exercise you should practice frequently at a trot and a canter as soon as you begin jumping. You should feel so well balanced and firm in the saddle that nothing your horse does makes you fall against him. Until you are able to canter easily without touching his neck or losing your balance, you should not try to jump without holding the mane.

2. When a horse refuses a jump:
   • You should stop him directly in front of the bar, facing it, then punish him with two or three smacks with your crop behind the saddle.
   • He should be brought into the jump again in exactly the same way.

Common mistakes:
   • Do not lose your temper.
   • You should not need to look back to see where you are hitting him. If you cannot coordinate holding him facing the jump and hitting him behind the saddle at the same time, practice the backward motion of your hand at a canter until you perfect the method.
   • You should not hit him so lightly that he is unbothered by it, nor so hard that it appears as if you *had* lost your temper.

You need to be precise in your punishment of a horse. Rewards and punishments are part of a horse's training, but if he makes mistakes, it is almost always the fault of the rider.

3. If your horse runs out on the second jump of an in and out
   • You should take him back to repeat both jumps.
   • As you are in the air over the first jump, you should be ready to turn him in the air to prevent him from running out again.
   • You should shorten up on the rein on the side on which he ran out the first time.

• Be sure you are thinking ahead to the second jump while you are still on the first jump.

Common mistakes:

• You should not let your horse lag as he approaches the jump so he does not have enough impetus for the jump.
• You should not look back or down as you go over the first jump.
• You should not let him run out again, because this indicates lack of control.
• You should not rush the jump.

4. When you jump a series of in and outs between two barriers, you do not need to work on control of your horse once he begins jumping. You need only to keep the impetus by pressing with your calves.

• Your form, therefore, should be correct over all the jumps.
• Your hands should move forward and backward with the movements of the horse's head, coming back into position as he touches the ground, moving up the sides of the neck again as he stretches for the next jump.
• You should feel how he times himself for the jump and go with him easily.

Common mistakes:

• If your form is incorrect for one of the jumps, you either failed to think ahead to the next jump, or you lost the sense of the horse's forward movement and were left behind.
• If you failed to bring your horse into the series of jumps, or failed to keep him jumping the entire set, you

did not make a correct approach or failed to have control of your horse.

This exercise is used to improve your form and to give you a feeling of how a horse times himself when he jumps. You should have a relaxed body, supple legs, and a sense of being with the horse. This is your stepping stone to following through with your hands when he jumps.

5. You should be able to jump 2½' using
    a. a bridge or half-bridge with your reins
    • You use the reins pressed across the horse's neck instead of holding the mane. This gives you more freedom of movement with your hands than holding the mane does.
    • You should be able to use a bridge without putting your weight against the neck on every jump.

Common mistakes:
    • You should not form a bridge with your reins incorrectly so that you pull on the bit as you rest the reins on your horse's neck.
    • You must not jerk on the reins for balance.
    • You should not have the reins so tight that they restrict your horse's free extension of his neck.

    b. an intermediate position with your hands touching either side of the neck.
    • You must be secure in your seat so you do not need your hands for balance.
    • You must have some sense of the feel of the horse's forward movement as he stretches his neck during the **jump.**

• You will not have contact with his mouth when your hands are resting on the neck.

Common mistakes:
• You should not interfere with your horse's movement by having your reins too short or failing to reach far enough forward on the neck as he jumps.
• Your form and control must not deteriorate while you concentrate on moving your hands forward to the neck while your horse is jumping.

It is most important not to snatch at your horse's mouth when you are putting your hands on the neck. If you cannot sit securely and remain at ease as you put your hands on the neck, continue to practice with your hands on the mane. It is better to gain a feel for jumping, the movement it takes, its demands on your position, than to strive for an intermediate position of your hands. This section of the test must be passed with confidence before you move on to the Blue Ribbon Test.

6. It takes "togetherness" to jump with a partner.
• You both must time your approach to have your horses shoulder to shoulder at the point when they should take off for the jump.
• You should have your horses close together.
• You should both stop your horses together at the end of the ring.
• You should both have the correct lead.

Common mistakes:
• If one of you makes a mistake, the other should keep close, even if it means walking, circling and approaching again.

• You should not blame your partner for any lack of control of his horse, but adjust your own horse to his pace and style.

• You must not forget your horse, how to time him, how to help him jump well, because you are thinking about two horses instead of one.

• You should not allow your horse to bite or kick.

You judge your proficiency for this section by how well the two horses look as a pair. If the horses act as if they were one, you have both ridden well. Your ability to control your horse under conditions that are not usual is tested here. Jumping with correct form should seem natural to you, so that you do not need to think of your position to jump well with a partner.

7. When you take a jump course in the woods

• Your horse should be under control as you approach each jump.

• After each jump you should bring your horse into a collected canter to direct him to the next jump.

• You should be prepared to turn toward the next jump while you are in the air over the previous jump. You should look in the direction you are planning to go so your horse will take the correct lead as he comes down from a jump.

• You should keep the proper distance from other jumpers.

• You should ride with confidence and expect your horse to be confident too.

Common mistakes:

• Control is the main challenge on an outside course. Your horse must not rush his jumps, nor refuse to move at a steady pace. You must not let your horse choose the direction and pace to take.

• If you fail to think ahead to the next jump, you will not take every jump correctly. You should not be left behind, interfere with your horse's movement on the jumps, nor lose your sense of form and balance.

• You should not become excited. A calm head means a calm course.

• You should not jerk your horse around.

You should be able to control a horse over a course without a fence nearby as an aid. This is an opportunity to prove you can think about several jumps at once. Your ability to collect a horse after a jump and push him for the next jump at the proper time is tested here.

8. You can spot a horse that is jumping too soon because he must reach as if stretching for a broader jump to get his forelegs across the bar. He often ticks the bar with his hind legs.

A horse that jumps too late often pauses before his take off. He will come very close to the bar. Often he ticks the bar with his forelegs. A horse that takes his jump in his stride will move naturally through the approach, take-off, flight and landing. There will be no abrupt movement.

17
Blue Ribbon Test

1. Have photographs taken of your jumping. Criticize these pictures to note your own faults.

2. Take your horse over a 3½′ jump.

*3. Demonstrate how to follow through with your hands on a jump.

*4. Demonstrate how to time a horse correctly for a jump.

*5. Jump a series of one-stride in and outs.

*6. Jump a course properly which has several different types of jumps including a chicken coop, a spread jump, a stone wall, and a jump that is new to you.

*7. Take a course in the woods or fields which has at least eight jumps, the highest of which is 3½′.

8. Take several different kinds of courses such as a figure eight and a diagonal.

HOW TO JUDGE YOUR PROFICIENCY ON THE BLUE RIBBON TEST

1. When you criticize photographs of your own jumping
   • Note correct form as well as mistakes in your position.

157

• Note how the horse has taken his jumps to see if you have motivated him correctly.

A picture of your jumping often helps you detect errors of which you were unconscious. It is a helpful tool to learning in every phase of riding.

2. There is no difference between a higher jump and lower one as far as motivating your horse and your own position are concerned.
 • You should be ready to absorb the shock of landing, which is harder on a higher jump. Your knees and ankles should be flexible.
 • Your seat must be secure, your heels down, so that you do not "fly" out of the saddle. You must grip with your calves.
 • Your horse should make a correct approach and move well after the jump.

Common mistakes:
 • You should have your horse alert so that he is not startled by the higher jump.
 • You should not interfere with your horse's head.
 • You should not fall back or forward on your horse.
 • You should not lose control of your horse before or after the jump.

Since different horses jump in different ways, you should take this jump on several types of horses to demonstrate how to deal with every kind of temperament.

3. The advanced position of your hands on a jump means your hands follow the movement of your horse's head.
 • Your seat must be secure and perfectly balanced.

- Your hands should move forward as the horse stretches his neck so that you allow him freedom of movement, yet you have light contact with his mouth.
- Your legs should not swing forward or backward, but should remain in the same place through approach, jump and landing.
- Your hands should be resilient so that you feel your horse's movement and follow it.

Common mistakes:

- You should never interfere with your horse's head by pulling on the reins.
- You *should* catch the mane to regain your balance if this will prevent you from jerking on your horse's mouth when something unexpected happens during jumping.

The ability to follow through with your hands should feel natural. You should be able to motivate your horse properly and hold your position when you demonstrate this skill.

4. When you demonstrate the correct way to time or "rate" your horse for a jump

- Bring your horse into the jump at a steady pace, moving alertly.
- You should know several steps before the jump if he is going to take it in his stride.
- You must feel with your horse, "riding" him, not just sitting on him, all through the approach and takeoff.
- If he needs to lengthen his stride in order to be placed correctly to take off for the jump, you should use leg pressure for each stride.

• If he needs to shorten his step to time the jump correctly, you apply tension on the reins for each step, even while you are urging him into the jump. This involves collecting him before the jump, then making certain he has his head *for* the jump.

Common mistakes:

• You must not think the horse will do all the work alone.

• If he is taking the approach correctly, you should not interfere with him.

• You cannot make a horse time his jumps well unless you can make him canter at the pace you ask, shorten or lengthen his stride, and take the jump when you direct.

• If your horse is not timed correctly for the jump by the last two or three strides, it is too late to change the length of his stride. You should not try.

In order to time your horse for a jump, you need to sense what he is thinking almost before he thinks it. You need a feel for his movement so you can tell whether he is pacing himself so that six strides or so will bring him to the natural takeoff point. Your approach should not be a fight with your horse; rather should it appear effortless. Timing a horse correctly is one of the most difficult phases of jumping.

5. The important thing to remember when taking a series of one-stride in and outs is to keep the motivation. By this time you should not need to think about form and can concentrate on your horse. You should move with your horse, having the feel of the downward touching of the forelegs followed immediately by the upward thrust

of the hindquarters that is associated with the horse reaching again with his head and neck, drawing your hands forward. Your movements should be perfectly timed with your horse's.

6. A well taken jump course has an even, smooth and effortless quality.
• When jumping a chicken coop, there should be willingness in your horse as he approaches it. It should not loom as a difficult obstacle.
• When taking a spread jump you should maintain your position longer in the air. Be careful not to interfere with his head.
• When jumping a stone wall, be prepared for a drop jump on the far side. You should not be jarred as you come down.
• A new type of jump should not worry you because you are so secure in your seat you can maintain your form over any obstacle. You have such control of your horse and he has such confidence in you there is no danger of his refusal. Still, be prepared for anything.
• When taking a course, you have control throughout. You are able to collect your horse after jumps by closing your legs and bringing your shoulder blades back. You are able to turn your horse in the air on a jump and land on the correct lead after each jump whichever direction the course turns.

You now know there is a lot to think about in the air over a jump: your position, the movement of your hands in contact with the horse's mouth, making him land correctly (using a squeeze if he appears he is going to jump too short), and thinking ahead for the next jump.

7. You should be able to take your horse over an outside course without difficulty in control, loss of position, or losing a feel for his mouth. The quality of your jumping, the lightness of your hands, the obedience of your horse, measure whether you pass this test.

8. A measure of your jumping skill is shown in how you take different types of courses.

• In a figure eight course you combine the skills of cantering a figure eight with those of jumping. Your lead will be changed when you change direction. Emphasis is placed on form, control and the appearance of ease with which you take the course. Your horse should not knock down the jumps (see diagram). A jump at the center of the eight is optional. If it is used it is jumped in both directions.

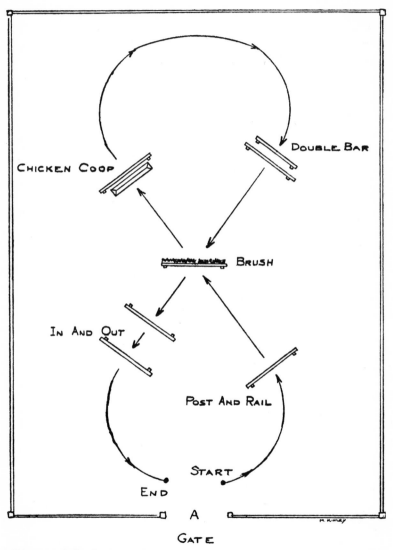

Figure eight jump course

• A course with jumps on either side, then a jump on the diagonal in the center, is another type of course you should know (see diagram).

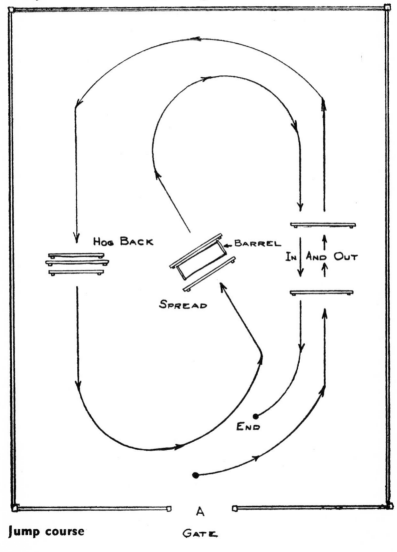

HOG BACK

BARREL

IN AND OUT

SPREAD

END

A

Jump course

GATE

Index

Advanced rider's tests, 85–129
Advantages of riding different
    horses, 40
Aged horse, 74, 81
Approaching a horse, 22
Arabian, 74, 81
Arms, position of, 24
Arrangement of tests, 11

Back of horse, 15, 21
Backing, 73, 76, 77, 113, 114
    controlled, 106, 116, 117
    mistakes, 77, 113, 114
    mistakes in controlled backing,
      116, 117
Balance, 17, 19, 24, 25, 27, 35,
    37, 62
    when changing diagonals, 75
    when jumping, 137, 138
    when trotting, 65
Ball of your foot, 24
Bareback, 73, 78, 79, 87–89
    balance, 79
    cantering, 101
    mistakes, 79, 88, 89
    mounting, 101
Bay, 74, 81
Beginning riders' tests, 15–42
Billets, 29, 31, 32
Bit, 15, 20, 21
Bridge of reins, 55, 63, 149, 153
Bridle(s), 20, 21, 29, 31, 32, 45,
    52–54
    checking a bridle, 65, 72
    importance of knowing how to,
      74, 84

Cannon bone, 93, 94
Canter(ing), 87, 89, 90, 115, 116,
    120, 149–151
    bareback, 101, 102
    figure eight, 119
    in a horse show, 111
    leads, 101, 102
    mistakes, 89, 90, 150
    mistakes cantering bareback,
      102, 103
    mistakes in leads, 104, 105
    reverse, 106

    steady, 106
    unwilling horse, 87, 90
    with partner, 126, 127
Cantle, 23, 27, 28
Care of a horse, 101, 102, 105, 119,
    127, 128
Change of direction, 73, 79–81
Changing gaits, 19
Cheek bone, 23, 28
Chestnut, 74, 81, 93, 94
Circle
    at a canter, 96, 99, 121, 126
    at a trot, 66, 87, 92, 93
    control as circle, 66
    in a group, 66, 67
    mistakes cantering a circle, 99
    mistakes trotting a circle, 66, 93
Clicking sound, 35, 39
Cooperative rider, 36, 74, 83, 120
Control, 17, 22, 36, 38, 47, 58, 91,
    96
    lack of, 31
    when circling, 66
    when jumping, 137, 138, 141
Coronet, 93, 94
Cow-kick, 22
Crest, 93, 94
Crop
    mistakes using a crop, 51
    using a crop, 45, 50, 51
Croup, 15, 21
Curb, 45, 52, 54
Cutting corners, 45, 51
    avoid, 48, 49

Diagonals, 64, 67, 96, 106
    balance when changing, 75
    changing, 73, 75, 115
    mistakes when changing, 75, 115
    on trail, 98
    reason for, 64, 71
Dismounting, 15, 55
    correctly, 17, 56, 57
    mistakes, 17, 57, 58
Distance from other horses, 74, 84
Double bridle, 45, 53, 54
Double reins, 45
    how to hold, 49

Elbow of horse, 93, 94